LISTENING TO BOB DYLAN

MUSIC IN AMERICAN LIFE

A list of books in the series appears at the end of this book.

LISTENING to
BOB DYLAN

LARRY STARR

**UNIVERSITY OF
ILLINOIS PRESS**
Urbana, Chicago, and Springfield

Library of Congress Cataloging-in-Publication Data
Names: Starr, Larry, author.
Title: Listening to Bob Dylan / Larry Starr.
Description: Urbana : University of Illinois Press, 2021. | Series: Music
    in American life | Includes bibliographical references and index.
Identifiers: LCCN 2021000396 (print) | LCCN 2021000397 (ebook) |
    ISBN 9780252043956 (cloth) | ISBN 9780252086021 (paperback) |
    ISBN 9780252052880 (ebook)
Subjects: LCSH: Dylan, Bob, 1941– —Criticism and interpretation. |
    Popular music—United States—Analysis, appreciation.
Classification: LCC ML420.D98 S73 2021 (print) | LCC ML420.D98 (ebook)
    | ddc 782.42164092—dc23
LC record available at https://lccn.loc.gov/2021000396
LC ebook record available at https://lccn.loc.gov/2021000397

CONTENTS

PREFACE

I have written this book as an admirer of Bob Dylan's work, and I picture you as another admirer, at least potentially. I'm not using the word *fan* here because, in these fraught times, the dividing line between fandom and fanaticism can get uncomfortably blurred. This is a book centered directly on the rich listening experience provided by Bob Dylan's musical performances. Dylan's huge output of commercially released recordings provides ample material for this purpose.

If you find yourself initially surprised by the notion that someone might actively love Bob Dylan's *music*, as opposed to loving just his lyrics or admiring his larger cultural importance, then please read on, because that notion lies at the core of my book's intent. I simply want to invite you metaphorically to sit down with me and listen to many remarkable songs, while I attempt to point out—without pretension and without the employment of musical jargon—both what is readily to be heard and what might be particularly worthy of your notice. By no means do I aim to provide purely objective, dry descriptions. I eagerly identify those elements I find to be effective, expressive, surprising, or moving in Dylan's songs and performances. I do not do so, however, with the expectation that you will necessarily share these specific reactions. I do so in the hope that you will find it worthwhile to understand the *possibility* of reacting to Dylan in such ways. Ideally, you might then be motivated to explore your own informed personal reactions to Dylan's work, venturing far beyond the very selective group of songs discussed in detail here.

With its focus on listening, this book might seem to belong within the category of what is called "music appreciation." This is a term I've long resisted, however, because it suggests a kind of distant respect for music, rather than the passionate, attentive love of music that I experience and that I always hope to convey to others. "Music appreciation" is also a term I've never before seen associated with discussions of Bob Dylan. Still, "music appreciation" is closer to what I'm attempting here than conventional conceptions of either music scholarship or music criticism, so I'll allow that term because "passionate, attentive love of music" (PALM?), while accurate, seems awkward and cumbersome. After too many years in academia, the last thing I would want to be is the author of an awkward and cumbersome book about Bob Dylan. It's worth remembering that a primary meaning of *appreciation* is gratitude, and gratitude is what this musician and listener feels for the musical artistry of Bob Dylan.

I want to offer reassurance here to anyone who might feel initially intimidated by material dealing with musical elements and musical form, and to any well-intentioned critics who might feel it is a mistake to include such material in a book intended primarily for nonspecialists. After more than five decades as a music educator, I can serve as my own witness to the fact that individuals without any formal training can readily hear the shape of a melody, prominent chord changes, rhythmic patterns, and basic musical form. I approach the treatment of these essential matters matter-of-factly, without presumptions or the use of specialists' language. The occasional technical term will be fully explained in context. Underestimating—or worse, condescending to—nonspecialists is a cultural offense that I have spent my entire career striving to avoid.

This book is organized conceptually, in terms of what I might call listening focus: turning detailed attention first to Bob Dylan's varied vocal styles, then to his harmonica playing, then to the compositional elements of his songs, then to his choices of instrumentation, and so forth. The inevitable result of this approach is that certain songs will appear in more than one chapter, considered from different listening standpoints. I hope that you will not find this distracting; in fact, it reflects my own listening habits, insofar as I enjoy returning to favorite songs, sometimes deliberately listening from a new perspective, and at other times being delightfully surprised by fresh aspects of something I had thought I thoroughly knew. The recurring songs are, intentionally, among Dylan's most celebrated and familiar ones, and I also hope that including them will make the book both more welcoming and more immediately useful to you. While I have leaned on the widely known songs, I have also made a deliberate attempt to include less-known songs that merit wider recognition in many of the chapters.

Bob Dylan's recorded work is voluminous, and I make no attempt here at inclusivity. If you find yourself thinking of additional songs that might have been discussed, or other good (or better) examples of the musical points under consideration, then that is very much what I'm aiming at. I even hope that the approaches to listening presented here might be found applicable to the work of other distinguished performing songwriters.

I have sought earnestly to avoid the pitfalls of writing excessively about myself, constantly offering my own opinions, and crossing that unmarked but sorely tempting borderline where aesthetic description shades into autobiography while Dylan's own work remains unilluminated. There has been far too much prose about Bob Dylan that appears to engage his work as a performing musician but offers only the occasional musical observation, while engaging fully with the author's personal reactions. Therefore I will not subject you to my own list of the forty best (or worst) Dylan songs, albums, outtakes, or whatever. I have never made such lists, nor have I seen the point of them, except as a means by which certain critics assert a level of expertise that belongs to nobody.

You will find nothing in these pages about the minutiae of Dylan's recording sessions, tour dates, or unofficial bootleg recordings. Neither will you discover arcana on the details of his personal life. Material of this sort is readily available elsewhere. Obscure unidentified references to Dylan's work and life, of the sort that plague so much of the published literature—functioning as childish, winking asides to others "in the know"—will have no place here. Neither will you be besieged with tales of my personal pilgrimages to iconic Dylan sites. In fact, I have never been to Hibbing, to Gerde's Folk City, or to Woodstock. I will assume that most likely you haven't either. And that disqualifies neither you nor me from appreciating Bob Dylan's work to the fullest. To quote the memorable title of a book by George Martin, the producer of the Beatles' recordings, "all you need is ears."

LISTENING TO BOB DYLAN

1
NOT BY WORDS ALONE

Bob Dylan won a Nobel Prize in 2016—for literature. This is now common knowledge. Still, it must be asked: Would anyone on the Nobel Prize jury even have heard of Bob Dylan were it not for his achievements as a performing songwriter?

Dylan himself articulated this paradox directly when he concluded his own Nobel lecture by observing that "songs are unlike literature. They're meant to be sung, not read. . . . And I hope some of you get the chance to listen to [my] lyrics the way they were intended to be heard: in concert or on record or however people are listening to songs these days." There is an ironic poignancy in these words, as the world-famous winner of one of the world's ultimate prizes humbly pleads with us at last just to *listen* to his work. This book will take Bob Dylan at his word: that is to say, not by words alone.

Consider the question "How does it feel?" By itself it's an everyday, unremarkable expression: one friend asking about another's emotional well-being; a salesperson hoping that the new shoes are fitting properly; a doctor or dentist assessing a patient's condition. Now imagine these same words being *sung* at you intensely by another person: "*How* does it *feeeeel*?" This is no longer that everyday question. Shaped by a familiar melody, rhythm, and vocal color, this can be one thing only, an evocation of Bob Dylan performing his iconic "Like a Rolling Stone."

That little exercise demonstrates something more than Bob Dylan's enormous impact on contemporary culture. It reveals the extent to which the very identity of Dylan's work is defined by music and musical performance. The words "How does it feel?" become "Like a Rolling Stone" only when Dylan's characteristic melody, rhythm, and vocal style are synthesized with them, becoming parts of an inseparable whole. The present book seeks to restore music and musical performance to their rightful positions, as central, essential aspects of Bob Dylan's art.

Long before he was awarded the Nobel Prize, the widespread tendency was to regard Bob Dylan primarily or even exclusively as a poet, or as a writer of lyrics. But Dylan's lyrics in isolation cannot properly represent his achievements or his work. "How does it feel?" provides a concise illustration. For a more substantial example, we might look to the 2006 edition of *The Oxford Book of American Poetry*, in which Dylan's arrival as a significant literary presence was certified with the appearance of his lyrics for "Desolation Row." The venerable anthology presents "Desolation Row" as a ten-stanza poem. But the presentation perpetrates a major distortion. The many listeners who have heard Dylan's own original recorded performance of "Desolation Row" on his celebrated album *Highway 61 Revisited* (1965) know it as a *twelve*-stanza *song*, two complete stanzas of which are played on Dylan's harmonica. The two missing stanzas are not so much as acknowledged in *The Oxford Book of American Poetry*. But does it make any sense to ignore two major sections of a major work simply because those sections are performed without words?

Music, no less than lyrics, deserves pride of place in any thorough consideration of song, and Dylan's art achieves its total impact only as a complete package—as a personal, unique synthesis of words, music, and performance. The mission of this book is to illuminate that complete package through the examination of readily available Dylan recordings.

It is necessary to rely on recordings, because the published Bob Dylan songbooks are as insufficient in their own way for this purpose as the anthologies of his lyrics. The songbooks simplify, sometimes drastically, the rhythmic and melodic freedom that characterizes Dylan's vocal performances and may omit some of his most colorful chord choices. The published vocal line for "Like a Rolling Stone" that appears in the so-called *Definitive Bob Dylan Songbook* hardly represents the varied ways Dylan sings that pivotal phrase "How does it feel?" Nor does that same *Songbook* offer a hint of the expressive, unusual, and dissonant guitar chord that accompanies the beginning of each vocal stanza in Dylan's original recorded performance of "Girl from the North Country" on the album *The Freewheelin' Bob Dylan* (1963).

There is, unfortunately, no Nobel Prize for songwriting. Song is an essential aspect of culture worldwide, and a prize in that area would clarify that song is a genre different from literature or musical composition; it is an art form of its own, drawing on elements of both, but distinct from either. Yet were Bob Dylan to have won a hypothetical Nobel for songwriting, that in itself would also have been insufficient, because his art is that of a *performing* songwriter. This is something yet again, contributing a third indispensable element to a distinctive, remarkable amalgam.

Bob Dylan, Musician: Singer, Instrumentalist, Composer

Bob Dylan is a singularly versatile and expressive singer, a man of many voices. He can be a chanting folksinger ("Masters of War") or a hectoring rock shouter ("Like a Rolling Stone") or a country crooner ("Lay, Lady, Lay"), and this list is just for starters. His voice can shape-shift, chameleon-like, from one track to the next on a single album. Is the energetic, amused narrator who sings the story-song "Lily, Rosemary and the Jack of Hearts" on the album *Blood on the Tracks* (1975) really the same person as the pain-struck, mournful vocalist on the immediately following track, "If You See Her, Say Hello"? And these two songs were recorded on the same day.

Dylan has employed his harmonica as yet another, alternative, "singing" voice throughout his long career. As an instrumentalist, he has also elected to use both acoustic and electric guitar in multiple ways. Sometimes he chose the piano rather than the guitar for certain songs, a choice that decisively influenced the expressive character of those selections; an essential contribution to the unusual dark mood created by "Ballad of a Thin Man" from the album *Highway 61 Revisited* is surely Dylan's hard-edged piano playing. Bob Dylan's song lyrics are vividly enhanced, colored, and even tweaked by his musical settings and performances, and vice versa, resulting in complex yet unified examples of songwriters' art.

Why is it then that we so often encounter claims that Bob Dylan has a "bad" voice, that he "can't really play" his instruments, or that his music by itself is "boring"? It is important to debunk the assumptions underlying such statements.

Admittedly, Bob Dylan does not possess what is typically called a "beautiful" voice. But there is a crucial difference between having a "beautiful" voice and being a distinguished singing *musician*. To assume that an attractive vocal instrument automatically produces beautiful music makes about as much sense as to assume that playing an exquisitely fashioned violin, or guitar, automatically renders the performer a fine musician. Conversely, generations of rural musicians have coaxed wonderful music from well-worn fiddles and banjos. If someone has "beautiful" hands, would we suppose her automatically to be a skilled craftsperson? It is important not to confuse a surface attractiveness with *artistic* beauty. Artistic beauty is a much deeper, more complex quality.

A very gifted young student of opera pleasantly surprised and educated me when she proclaimed Bob Dylan a "great singer" and offered in explanation, "It's not the instrument you have, it's what you *do* with your instrument." I can see no way to improve on that formulation.

Many of the most remarkable and influential singers of twentieth-century popular music did not possess inherently "beautiful" voices. Perhaps the obvious and outstanding example is Louis Armstrong, a great singing musician who was capable of "playing" his voice with the same expressiveness and imagination with which he played his trumpet. Billie Holiday had an idiosyncratic vocal instrument with a limited range, but she employed it to create performances of enduring poignancy. And the singer whom every creator of the "Great American Songbook"—Irving Berlin, George Gershwin, Cole Porter, and others—most wanted to perform his songs? That was Fred Astaire, a man with a "small," not obviously distinguished voice, who could also draw from his dancing vocabulary a feeling for vocal rhythm and phrasing second to none.

Similar reasoning applies in evaluating Bob Dylan, not only as a vocalist, but as an instrumentalist. I have spoken with skilled musicians who have spent productive lifetimes working in popular idioms, and they all offer slight variations on the same idea: that Dylan may be an idiosyncratic guitarist, harmonica player, and pianist, but his instrumental work is inevitably well suited to the purposes of his songs and that work is powerfully effective as he employs it. The musical distinction of Bob Dylan's performances on all his instruments, including his voice, will be demonstrated with many examples in the chapters to follow.

Now what about Dylan's *music* itself? Are the songs of any interest if divested of their lyrics? The notion that his music is "boring," or lacking in some other way, in and of itself will set us off on a track that is irrelevant to a consideration of his songs as integrated wholes. But besides that, the notion, as a wholesale generalization, is simply not true.

The specific characterization of Dylan's music as boring appears in print at least as far back as 1982, in a book by Betsy Bowden called *Performed Literature: Words and Music by Bob Dylan* (second edition, 2001). Dr. Bowden surely deserves recognition insofar as hers is one of the earliest books to consider Dylan seriously as a performer—although the word *literature* in her title warns, accurately, of trouble ahead. The "boring" complaint comes on the first page, but it is never clear exactly to what she is referring. To perform Dylan's songs without words, substituting one or more instruments for the vocals, is to present them as they were never intended to be heard. It is bad enough to hear the Beatles' "Eleanor Rigby" as elevator music, but just to imagine "A Hard Rain's a-Gonna Fall" in that guise is sufficient to ruin an entire day. Nevertheless, Dylan has written some memorable melodies; "Mr. Tambourine Man" is a well-known example. If, however, Bowden means that the accompaniments to Dylan's sung melodies are musically uninteresting, her criticism has yet less validity. Even song accompaniments by the greatest composers of art songs—Schubert, Schumann, Brahms, and others—can seem uninteresting, or even incoherent, if divorced from the vocal lines they were designed to partner.

On the other hand, there are Dylan songs in which the music is the *most* interesting aspect of the whole. The lyrics to the song "You're a Big Girl Now," from *Blood on the Tracks*, are essentially a collection of clichés (including the song's title). Here are the opening lines:

> Our conversation was short and sweet.
> It nearly swept me off-a my feet.

This scarcely seems Nobel Prize–worthy literature. What more than redeems the lyrics, however, is the underlying music, which employs two chords that are totally unexpected—first, in terms of their relationship to the home key established by the instrumental introduction, and second in terms of their relationship to the vocal line itself. There are more traditional choices of chords that might be paired with the opening vocal melody, but "You're a Big Girl Now" is not a three-chord song. (Dylan could vary the chord choices in live performances of the song, as the 1976 album *Hard Rain* documents.)

In "You're a Big Girl Now," the sense that there is something amiss is deliberate, of course. It allows the music to foreshadow an emotional coloring that becomes apparent in the lyrics only later: the word *sweet* is actually being employed ironically, and the singer has been "swept" off his feet not by a rush of positive feelings, but because he has literally been dumped by the "big girl." There are many such instances in Dylan's work, where the music is doing the heaviest lifting to project the deeper meanings of the song.

Exhibit A: "Like a Rolling Stone"

Bob Dylan as vocalist, as instrumentalist, and as composer are all on splendid display in his original 1965 recording of "Like a Rolling Stone." This performance has been so widely heard, discussed, and celebrated that it is difficult to move it beyond the comfortable status of an old favorite. "Like a Rolling Stone" is most likely a song that we enjoy recognizing, but to which we no longer pay much serious attention. While really *listening* to this record again, as if for the first time, may prove a challenge, it is a worthwhile undertaking. If we make the effort to defamiliarize ourselves with "Like a Rolling Stone," the radical artistry of Dylan's performance may reassert itself to the forefront of awareness.

It is useful to separate out particular high points of musical performance in "Like a Rolling Stone" for examination, but such a process inevitably leads to a certain artificiality, since vocals, instruments, and compositional choices were all intertwined in the creation of such a recording. The lyrics are of necessity involved as well; it makes no more sense to exclude them from consideration than it does to discuss the lyrics independently of the music. I will attempt to deal with these complexities as gracefully as possible, remaining aware of the severe limitations that accompany any attempt to describe musical experience in prose. By no means will a complete analysis—if there could ever be such a thing—be the goal. I will point out certain prominent features of the recording, hopefully encouraging the reader to discover many other analogous features, and allowing space to uncover much else that doubtless has eluded my own attention.

To begin at the beginning, was there ever an opening vocal line for a song that commences as innocently and ends up as accusingly as this one? "Once upon a time," sung on a repeated note, seems momentarily noncommittal. But all too rapidly, further repeated notes, intoned by Dylan like accelerating hammer strokes, achieve their finger-pointing impact. This is not simply a matter of lyrics; it is all about sung rhythm, and the effect is something like this:

Once upon a time you dressedsofine, youthrewthebumsadime inyourprime

And then, an uncomfortably long pause, to allow the developing verbal and musical tone of the song to register for a moment, prior to the wallop of a punchline: "didn't you?" Here, for the first time, the vocal line leaps up in pitch, with Dylan maximizing the change through increased volume and heavy accentuation. In terms of both music and lyrics, the opening idea could have ended with "in your prime." With "didn't you?" that opening idea abruptly becomes a question rather than a statement, and the melody line is left hanging in the air just as the aggressive question in the lyrics aims a metaphoric poisoned arrow. This is one of those moments that can never be more effective than it is in the surprise upon our initial hearing of it—although, to be sure, it retains its punch with repeated listenings.

The opening vocal line of "Like a Rolling Stone" presents in miniature Dylan's basic strategies for building the entire six-minute song. Musically, the repetition of individual notes, then of vocal phrases, and then of entire stanzas, is given impetus, variety, and intensification by means of Dylan's vocal delivery. Leaps up or down in the melodic line occur sporadically on important words, the upward leaps underlined by strong vocal accents. Bob Dylan employs his voice as a powerful *rhythm* instrument, as well as a pitch instrument. And the savvy employment of pauses in the line proves a source of both tension and release as the song progresses. The first vocal phrase is unique in that it turns what could have been a finished statement into a question. Later phrases utilize pauses to make us wait anxiously for what we know must be significant endings to ideas. A ready example is provided by the opening of the second stanza, with music directly parallel to that which opens the first:

Ah, you've gone to the *fin*-est school, all right, MissLonely, butyouknowyouonlyusedtoget . . . JUICED IN IT!

Before proceeding with some additional examination of Dylan's art-istry in "Like a Rolling Stone," I should acknowledge that I didn't actually begin at the beginning. Dylan's vocal entrance is preceded by a striking instrumental introduction, starting with a drum stroke and prominently featuring both organ and piano. It was an extraordinary sound for its time, and it's important to remember that it was Dylan's own choice—part of his compositional process, the academics might say—to employ such a large ensemble and to have it open the performance. It's as if a dense, even overpowering, musical environment is introduced, providing a background of near-chaotic intensity, over which Dylan's voice nevertheless predomi-nates as he denounces pretension and hypocrisy. That his voice can in fact predominate is a tribute to his vocal prowess and expressiveness. It is also, however, a tribute to the role played by expert engineering and production in the making of this recording, a role that should never be underestimated. We know from accounts of those present at the recording session that Dylan had some input into these aspects as well, insisting early on, for example, that the organ be more prominent in the mix.

In its overall structure, "Like a Rolling Stone" consists of four long stan-zas, each of which presents a verse-chorus arrangement; the choruses are invariably introduced with the essential question "How does it feel?" Within the stanzas, the chorus is linked to the verse lyrically and musically by means of a simple but ingenious device. Each verse proceeds with musical phrases in pairs, the musical repetitions underlined by lyric rhymes: in the first stanza, didn't you/kiddin' you; laugh about/hangin' out; talk so loud/seem so proud. The pattern is broken, however, with the unpaired long line immediately preceding the chorus ("about having to be scrounging your next meal"), which hangs unresolved on a long note. The subsequent onset of the chorus presents simultaneously the resolving chord and the missing rhyme ("feel" rhyming, in this case, with "meal"). This, in turn, initiates a musical string of similar brief phrases that continue and conclude the chorus, all tied together with a series of rhyming words (home/unknown/stone).

Stanzas two, three, and four follow a plan analogous to that of the first, with a single modification. In the second stanza, the chorus is extended for one additional brief phrase, and the rhymes become: own/home/unknown/stone. This alteration adds to the already high level of intensity and sets the pattern for the remaining two stanzas. Whatever Dylan's reasons for introducing this change into the second chorus of "Like a Rolling Stone," the revised words provided his admirers with a memorable phrase. "No direction home" became the title of Robert Shelton's widely admired 1986 biography of Dylan and was later the title of the 2005 Martin Scorsese documentary.

It is easy, perhaps too easy, to state that each stanza of this song is sung to the same music. In the case of Bob Dylan's performance, the word *same* should be replaced by *similar*. *Same* obscures the many variations in rhythm, specific note choices, volume, and vocal color that animate Dylan's performance as he proceeds from stanza to stanza in "Like a Rolling Stone" (and in so many of his other performances). Consider, for instance, the way in which the words immediately preceding the choruses—meal, deal, steal, conceal—are delivered by Dylan with a ferocity that increases with each stanza. Notice as well how he finds different ways to lean on the recurring "feel," sometimes turning it virtually into a two-syllable word: *fee-*el. And, just when it seems that the vitriol in Dylan's voice could not possibly increase further, the final "How does it feel?" in the last stanza is enhanced with a preceding "Ah," as if metaphorically giving the knife an additional twist.

Dylan plays guitar throughout the recording of "Like a Rolling Stone," but it is the brief appearances of his harmonica that represent his most striking instrumental contribution to the performance. Dylan's harmonica is heard only during the breaks between the stanzas. Since the harmonica is not present at all during the instrumental introduction, its first appearance immediately after stanza one may come as a well-timed surprise. And the initial appearance is here and gone so quickly it seems almost like a tease, the musical equivalent of a lick and a promise. After that, the harmonica reappears regularly, playing a structural role in the song, but it suddenly becomes more insistent in the break between the third and final stanzas, completely dominating the foreground at that point. The process culminates in the concluding instrumental fade-out, with the harmonica at full blast and apparently now reluctant to relinquish the stage. From an expressive standpoint, it is as if the harmonica is mercilessly razzing and mocking "Miss Lonely," the unfortunate woman who is the object of the singer's scorn.

A fuller appreciation of the harmonica's contribution to this performance may come from listening to the rejected take of the song that is heard on

The Best of the Cutting Edge, volume 12 in *The Bootleg Series*, disc 1, track 15. Despite the information in the compilation's accompanying booklet, no harmonica is heard at all on this alternative version, and the track is arguably the weaker for it (although, like many rejected takes now available on such officially released bootleg recordings, it does present interesting variants in Dylan's vocal phrasing and delivery).

"Like a Rolling Stone" admirably exemplifies Bob Dylan's artistry as a vocalist, as an instrumentalist, and as a songwriting composer. More than that, it reveals the extent to which his lyrics, his music, his singing, and his playing are all bound together in the creation of an appropriately celebrated whole that is so much more than the mere sum of its parts.

2

FOLKSINGER, BLUESMAN, ROCKER, CROONER

The Many Voices of Bob Dylan

Bob Dylan is the straightforward title of his first album, released in 1962, and from the first track it is evident that this performer is no traditional folksinger. His interpretation of Jesse Fuller's "You're No Good" revels in vocal idiosyncrasies: a nasal tone, a breakneck pace, sudden variations in volume, words rushed together followed closely by elongated vowels ("nobodyintheworld can get along withyouuu," "well yougimmethe-bluues, I guess you're satisfiiiied"), a barely suppressed laugh (just before and at the end of the line "you wouldn't even let me in"), a growl in the voice ("jumpin' all over me," and many times thereafter)—all this and more in a performance that lasts considerably less than two minutes. It demonstrates unequivocally that Dylan wanted to present himself as a distinctive "voice" from the outset. Jesse Fuller's own performances of the song took a much more relaxed tempo and employed a much more consistent vocal style. Regardless of whether one hears "You're No Good" as a tour-de-force vocal debut or as an incoherent collection of self-conscious vocal mannerisms, or as something else entirely, it is clearly the work of a performer determined not to be ignored. For that reason, it functions as a signpost to Dylan's ambitions and methods.

The entire first album, a distinctive collection of eleven folk standards and two original songs ("Talkin' New York" and "Song to Woody"), retains considerably more than archival interest. While naturally indicative of how Dylan started out as a performing musician, the skills and proclivities in evidence here decisively informed his future efforts. The album will serve as a useful point of reference for this and succeeding chapters of this book.

When Bob Dylan began his performing and recording career, the vocal style commonly associated with folksinging was like that of Pete Seeger. Seeger employed an unmannered, conversational approach to song, devoid of any regional accents or self-consciously artistic effects. By far the most popular of the so-called "folksingers" at this time were the Kingston Trio, whose vocal approach essentially mirrored that of Seeger. Following in their footsteps were Peter, Paul, and Mary, who were the first artists to turn Bob Dylan songs into mainstream hit records, with "Blowin' in the Wind" and "Don't Think Twice, It's All Right" (both 1963). In this context, Dylan's singing would be, and indeed was, heard as eccentric. Less genteel terms were also applied. Dylan himself made his initial reception a source of humor in "Talkin' New York," the album track immediately following "You're No Good"; he tells of club owners rejecting him because he sounded like a "hillbilly": "We want *folksingers* here."

Dylan's basic model at this early time in his career was in fact the celebrated Oklahoma hillbilly singer and songwriter Woody Guthrie. Guthrie had been a prominent figure in the urban New York City–centered folk-music culture since the early 1940s, when he was a member of the Almanac Singers, along with Pete Seeger. While Guthrie was surely an anomalous presence in that culture, this factor worked in his favor, as his rural, "hard travelin'" background made him prized for his authenticity. Guthrie had for a long time been sidelined by debilitating illness when Bob Dylan arrived in New York City in 1961, and, despite (or possibly, to some degree, because of) his vocal idiosyncrasies, Dylan came to be regarded by many as Guthrie's heir, and consequently as a folksinger. But Dylan in his own way was as anomalous a folk artist as Guthrie. Like his model, Dylan from the start was a restless, searching creative figure, and Dylan's evolution eventually tore him away from the very circles that had embraced and enabled him early on. His restlessness was foreshadowed by the variety of vocal styles, and the often aggressive singing, heard on his first album.

First, to consider the Woody Guthrie influence. Guthrie's vocal phrasing and southwestern regional accent is mimicked directly by Dylan in his performances of the two self-composed songs on *Bob Dylan*, and elsewhere on that album as well. "Talkin' New York" is modeled clearly on Guthrie's spoken "talking blues" numbers (such as "Talking Hard Work" and "Mean Talking Blues"), and "Song to Woody" borrows the melody line, formal structure, and even the specific phrasing of Guthrie's "1913 Massacre." As Dylan became increasingly a performer of his own songs, his "Guthrie voice" became a central performing focus for a while, as may be heard on the albums *The Freewheelin' Bob Dylan* (1963) and *The Times They Are a-Changin'* (1964).

However natural Woody Guthrie's singing voice may have been to its owner, the inescapable fact is that it was by no means natural to Bob Dylan, who was born and raised in Minnesota, far from Guthrie's Oklahoma. Dylan's voice on "Talkin' New York," like the very different voice heard on "You're No Good," is, in effect, a kind of vocal mask donned by the performer, even though one might expect him to employ his natural voice for a song of his own creation, a number that is obviously describing his personal experiences. But one would be hard put to determine, on the basis of the eclectic vocal approaches that characterize his first album, what Dylan's natural singing voice might actually be. This eclecticism, taking the form of various vocal masks, seems to me nevertheless an essential aspect of Dylan's vocal presentation, and not just early on; the observation applies to a significant extent throughout much of his career. I do not intend *mask* as a pejorative term. Rather, it is an artistic strategy. And Bob Dylan is much more of a conscious artist than he is often assumed to be. His singing can perhaps be excessively self-conscious too, but this is a manifestation of his conscientiousness.

The concept of masking, and the related concept of a fluid, or even a concealed, identity could readily be seen as defining elements of Dylan's entire public presentation. From early on, he fashioned multiple and contradictory tall tales about his background and youthful experiences. At a concert performance on Halloween evening, 1964, Dylan told his audience that he was "masquerading," wearing his "Bob Dylan mask." (A recording of the concert is available, released in 2004 as volume 6 of *The Bootleg Series, Bob Dylan Live 1964: Concert at Philharmonic Hall*, and the front cover of the CD booklet shows Dylan in front of a pegboard prominently displaying three masks.) The mask quip, while doubtless intended to be a joke appropriate for the occasion, may appear in retrospect as foreshadowing: as Dylan's career advanced, so did his donning of various Bob Dylan masks. His fondness for wearing sunglasses, the periodic striking changes in his dress and appearance, his employment of whiteface during his Rolling Thunder tours of 1975 and 1976—all are well-documented manifestations of Dylan's many masks. In the 1973 movie *Pat Garrett and Billy the Kid*, Dylan portrayed a character named Alias, and his own 2003 film, in which he played the rock star Jack Fate, bore the title *Masked and Anonymous*. Throughout the 2000s, Dylan has produced his own albums under the pseudonym Jack Frost. And Dylan has always guarded his private and family life carefully, successfully keeping it from the public eye to an extent remarkable for a world-famous figure of his time. There is a great deal that might be thought and written about all this, but the important point for the listener to Dylan's recordings is that his adaptation of multiple vocal identities is reflective of encompassing, ongoing strategies that have marked this artist's entire public career.

Attributing strategies, with its implication of very conscious intent, to a performer like Bob Dylan may seem to open a host of problematic issues. Great care should always be taken when attributing conscious intent to most artists, and this applies to no artist more than Dylan, whose many interviews and public statements—performances themselves—typically offer no real assistance in gauging his artistic intentions. Indeed, these performances often appear designed to mystify and even mislead the public, which raises the issue of intent yet again. In any and all meanings of the words, Bob Dylan is a fabulous fabulist. What is apparent, however, just from a consideration of the first two songs on his first professional recording, is that Dylan is a performing musician who understood from early on exactly what he was doing, a savvy performer with a highly developed feeling for the effect and intelligence of his musical choices. Doubtless both on-the-spot inspiration and carefully considered calculation had their roles to play in the development of Dylan's artistry, but the finest artists have the gift of making choices that might be profoundly premeditated appear to be utterly spontaneous.

Returning now to Dylan's vocal masks, what kind of mask defines the Dylan introducing himself to a listening public with Jesse Fuller's "You're No Good"? Fuller was an African American performer with rural roots, and many of the vocal effects employed in Dylan's rendition of Fuller's song, such as idiosyncratic diction and growling, are common characteristics in the work of black country blues artists. One very distinctive aspect of Dylan's first album, setting it apart from the work of most of his contemporaries active in the folk culture of the early 1960s, is the extent to which it relies both on black blues sources and on the vocal techniques associated with those sources. And Dylan's use of these techniques in his interpretations can be more extreme than is typical even of performances by the songs' creators; this is obviously the case not just with the Fuller song, but with Bukka White's "Fixin' to Die" on the same album. Where White's own recording of the song projects a darkly resigned character, Dylan is frenetic, desperate, raging. Dylan may employ blues-style vocals on songs that are not typically sung in that fashion. One example from the first album is the spiritual "Gospel Plow" and another, from white country sources, is "Freight Train Blues." (In the case of Dylan's "Gospel Plow," it is illuminating to compare it with Pete Seeger's measured and straightforward performance of "Keep Your Eyes on the Prize," presumably the same song, which may be heard on Seeger's 1963 album *We Shall Overcome*.)

For Bob Dylan, from the beginnings of his recording career, the country blues constituted an essential and wide-ranging presence in his DNA as a singer. The enduring importance of the country blues repertoire for Dylan is reflected in his striking return to it over three decades later, on two albums of solo acoustic performances. These albums, *Good As I Been to You* (1992) and *World Gone Wrong* (1993), mix black country blues standards with other old songs, chiefly from British sources (as was "Pretty Peggy-O" from Dylan's first album). It is no surprise that Dylan became also a major writer of original blues.

"You're No Good," "Gospel Plow," and "Freight Train Blues" are all remarkable for their frantic pacing, along with their blues-based vocal stylings. Where did Dylan get the inspiration to perform at such speeds? Surely not from traditional folk sources or the performances typical of his contemporary folksingers. I suggest it was from his teenage love of rock 'n' roll, particularly the mid- to late-1950s hit recordings of Little Richard, and those of Elvis Presley at his most aggressive; Richard and Presley were early idols of Dylan. Indeed, "Highway 51" on *Bob Dylan* borrows its signature guitar riff directly from the Everly Brothers' rock 'n' roll hit "Wake Up Little Susie" (1957), vastly accelerating the tempo of that source. In his "Highway 51," Dylan showcases a shouting, growling vocal that clearly anticipates the rocker voice he later unleashed fully in songs like "Maggie's Farm" on *Bringing It All Back Home* (1965), Dylan's first album to utilize rock instrumentation. This is the rocker voice that Dylan went on to employ so effectively on the soon-to-follow "Like a Rolling Stone." "Highway 51" is arguably already a rock performance, lacking only bass and drums.

Other songs on Dylan's first album are representative of the more conventional folk repertoire of the times, such as "Man of Constant Sorrow," "Pretty Peggy-O," and "House of the Risin' Sun." In these, elements of his Guthrie-inflected singing style are prominent, along with other interpretive nuances probably borrowed from other singers Dylan was hearing on records and in clubs at the time. Dave Van Ronk's performance of "House of the Risin' Sun" was a very specific influence.

A singing, songwriting, and performing heir to Woody Guthrie; a developing, passionate bluesman; an embryonic rocker—all but one of the major personae that would define Dylan as a vocalist over the next decade are to be heard on his debut recording. The one important mask not assumed is that of crooner. It would take nearly a decade for this one to appear on records (*Nashville Skyline*, 1969, and *Self Portrait*, 1970), and its appearance created no end of surprise and consternation. It is worth noting, however, that friends from Dylan's Minnesota days recalled hearing the emerging performer use a decidedly delicate vocal approach, and they experienced their own great surprise at the "New York" voice(s) revealed on *Bob Dylan*. Perhaps his entire vocal arsenal was present, at least in budding form, from the beginning.

Heir to Woody Guthrie

With the first song on his second album, *The Freewheelin' Bob Dylan* (1963), Dylan pays ample tribute to his idol in both songwriting and performance—not through straightforward imitation, as in the earlier "Song to Woody," but through the creation of significantly original work that builds on Guthrie's strong foundation. Like Guthrie's own best songs, "Blowin' in the Wind" employs homely, functional musical material to project seemingly homespun lyrics of immediate contemporary relevance and enduring power. The four-line stanzas of "Blowin' in the Wind" present lyrics in a verse-refrain arrangement, where the final line of each stanza follows three questions with the assertion that "The answer is blowin' in the wind." This simple pattern recurs precisely over the course of the three-stanza song, resulting in an immediately accessible form, suitable for ready memorization and sing-alongs. The melody line is gently lilting, repetitive but memorable, in the fashion of much folk music; as is the case with Guthrie's work, and with much folk music as well, the melody is evocative of a preexisting source, in this case the spiritual "No More Auction Block." The lyrics allude to the concerns of Dylan's early-1960s audience in addressing the fear of war (the Cold War between the United States and the Soviet Union was at its height at this time) and the burgeoning civil-rights movement ("How many years can some people exist before they're allowed to be free?"). Arguably Dylan goes a step beyond Guthrie's political songs by framing his lyrics so that they are less specifically tied to the time of their creation and expressive of more wide-ranging, unfortunately timeless, concerns.

"Blowin' in the Wind" is so celebrated and familiar that to return to the original recording of it, and listen with fresh ears, can provide a bracing experience. Dylan's is a stark, utterly unpretentious performance, possessing something like the piercing intensity of a black-and-white Walker Evans photograph from the Depression era. The guitar strums simply, allowing Dylan's voice to dominate without strain. Dylan underlines with accents and rhythmic syncopation the critical words in each of the song's questions, culminating in the final, deeply troubling one: "<u>How</u> many <u>deaths</u> will it <u>take</u> till he <u>knows</u> that <u>too many people</u> have <u>died</u>?"

The extent to which Dylan's voice can function in a rhythmic capacity to enhance expressivity and meaning is both significant and underappreciated. The careful, speech-like pacing and accentuation are characteristics that Dylan readily absorbed from the recordings of Woody Guthrie, but Dylan's employment of this approach goes considerably further than would be typical of Guthrie. As is the case with the vocal techniques that Dylan derived from blues sources, he seems determined to go beyond his model in order to achieve an impact on the listener both distinctive and powerful.

The rhythmic impact of Dylan's performance may be readily appreciated by comparing his recording of "Blowin' in the Wind" with that by Peter, Paul, and Mary, whose version achieved enormous popular success. With the folk group, everything is smooth and soothing: long, rounded vowel sounds; an avoidance of aggressive accents; words flowing gracefully one to another from the beginnings to the endings of phrases. The rhythm is predictable: on-the-beat singing, without syncopation. If the goal was to popularize Dylan's song by "mainstreaming" it, the Peter, Paul, and Mary record obviously met that goal, in no small measure by adhering to the folk-style norms of the period. Whether this approach best serves the meaning of the song, or makes the listener feel the importance of the song, is a different matter.

Clearly Dylan does not want *his* listener to feel comfortable listening to his own "Blowin' in the Wind." His vocal tone is anything but soothing, especially compared with Peter, Paul, and Mary. His sung rhythms are jagged, with syncopated accents from the outset ("How many <u>roads</u> must a <u>man</u> walk <u>down</u> . . .," and many other examples), and abrupt cutoffs ("in the wind" at the end of each stanza, the phrase nearly becoming a single word, dropped unceremoniously to avoid any sense of a comfortable resolution). Beginning with the third question in the lyrics, Dylan opens his phrases with a rhythmically awkward "yes 'n'," a deliberately destabilizing touch, as if he is buttonholing the listener, forcing attention on the successive queries. Dylan's voice can function in effect as a pitched percussion instrument, as well as a traditional melody instrument. The importance of rhythm in this performance is reinforced by the suddenly aggressive, rapid guitar strums that conclude the track, as if providing a series of musical exclamation points to further jolt the listener.

One essential element of Dylan's "Blowin' in the Wind" will remain unexamined for the moment: the harmonica interludes that follow each sung stanza. The harmonica plays a role so important in Bob Dylan's work that it demands its own chapter, proceeding directly after this one, in which it will be considered as the singer's other voice.

Dylan's "Guthrie singing voice" is heard prominently in most of the songs on *The Freewheelin' Bob Dylan*, and he offers another original Guthrie-style "talking blues" on this album as well ("Talkin' World War III Blues"). His evocation of Guthrie's specific regional accent became somewhat less consistent on his next album, *The Times They Are a-Changin'* (1964). Nevertheless, Woody Guthrie's characteristic approach to pacing and phrasing—both lyrically and musically—finds ready echoes in Dylan's work throughout *The Times They Are a-Changin'*, and that approach continued to exercise a major influence on Dylan for a long time.

After his mid-1960s phase as an electric rocker, and a period of recuperation from a motorcycle accident, Dylan returned to acoustic guitar (adding bass and drums) with *John Wesley Harding* late in 1967. "I Am a Lonesome Hobo" from that album demonstrates Guthrie's enduring influence: a simple, three-stanza structure; unpretentious lyrics with an unambiguous moral message; a melody line that closely follows the pacing, phrasing, and accent patterns of the lyrics; and a vocal performance that underlines these characteristics of the melody throughout. The song's avoidance of lyrical ambiguity keeps it closer to the spirit of Guthrie than many of the other songs on this often cryptic, darkly colored album, although it's doubtful Guthrie would have painted any hobo in as unflattering a light.

Personalizing the Blues

The term *blues* has been used for a very wide range of song forms and performance styles, ranging from the "talking blues" of Woody Guthrie to the work of black country artists such as Bukka White, Blind Willie Johnson, and Blind Lemon Jefferson, all of whom recorded songs performed by Bob Dylan on his first album. Blues has had a correspondingly wide-ranging influence on Dylan as both songwriter and performer. It is also important to realize that Dylan sometimes placed the word *blues* in the titles of songs that, strictly speaking, are blues neither in musical form nor in performance style. This is true, for example, of "North Country Blues" from *The Times They Are a-Changin'*, where *blues* is used in a very general sense, simply to refer to a melancholy or pessimistic mood.

The focus here will be on those elements derived from the vocal techniques of black country artists that Dylan utilized in performing his own songs, as he moved beyond the emulation stage represented by his first album. There is the strong rhythmic emphasis (heard clearly in Dylan's interpretation of Bukka White's "Fixin' to Die"); a close attention to phrasing, pacing, and accentuation characterized Woody Guthrie's vocals as well as those of country blues singers, and this aspect of performance reveals a link between two central influences on Dylan. There are also two distinct approaches to vocal melody gleaned by Dylan from blues sources. One approach involves the focusing of a phrase on a single repeated note, ornamented here and there with adjacent or nearby scale pitches above or below it—a kind of chanting, somewhat akin to intoned speech. The other approach is the diametric opposite of the first, a vocal flexibility that employs sliding between adjacent pitches on a single syllable. These techniques are in evidence on the most blues-inflected track from *The Freewheelin' Bob Dylan*, "Down the Highway."

The opening phrases of Dylan's "Down the Highway" exemplify the chanting just described, first on a relatively high note (*"walkin' down the high*-[way]"), then on a lower note ("with my *suitcase in my hand*"). This pattern is found throughout the song. Elsewhere, Dylan's vocal melody slides expressively among pitches ("I really miss my ba-*by-y-y*"; "the way I love that wo-*ma-a*-n"; and climactically in the last stanza, "walkin' down your high-wa-*y-y-y*," with his voice going into a strained falsetto). Other characteristics derived from country blues are the very informal diction and an almost improvisatory approach to rhythm. A musician would not be able to notate

Dylan's performance accurately within a fixed written meter, and a listener would have difficulty tapping her foot steadily at many points during the recording. Such flexibility, readily feasible in a solo acoustic context, would seem inimical to a successful band performance, but a fascinating aspect of Dylan's development is his gradual, increasing incorporation of rhythmic irregularities into songs he performs with a band. This will receive some attention in chapter 4.

"Bob Dylan's Blues," another track from *Freewheelin'*, is actually less bluesy than "Down the Highway," but it does share the vocal exaggerations and exuberant tempo of "You're No Good" and other selections from Dylan's first album. "Bob Dylan's Blues" is also characterized by chant-like vocals, but this technique became such a foundational element in Dylan's songwriting, as well as his singing, that it presents us with a conundrum. Does this blues-derived technique simply meld into Dylan's encompassing identity as an artist, so that its specific origins come to seem no longer of great import? Or is it more fitting to see the mature Bob Dylan as a bluesman to the core, with the other elements of his artistry circling around the blues foundations like planets around the sun? The importance of vocal sliding, and of rhythmic intensity and flexibility, to Dylan throughout his career—elements also traceable directly to his engagement with the blues—presents the same conundrum.

If we resolve the issue by deciding to call Bob Dylan a bluesman, this in turn might illuminate his relatively free use of the term *blues* in the titles of his songs, particularly some from the mid-1960s. Examples would be "Just Like Tom Thumb's Blues" from *Highway 61 Revisited* (1965) and "Stuck Inside of Mobile with the Memphis Blues Again" from *Blonde on Blonde* (1966), neither of which exhibits what musicians would call a typical blues form. (Blues as a form will be discussed in chapter 5.) The former song, however, has a chanting vocal line of a type that had become characteristic of Dylan by this time, along with pitch sliding that is especially marked on rhyming words (and that helps call them to attention). And "Stuck Inside of Mobile with the Memphis Blues Again" offers a vocal performance that remarkably synthesizes a kind of speech-song with abundant sliding, particularly in the song's chorus ("Oh, Mama, can this really be the end"). Dylan's fluid approach to rhythm is evident in both songs. Analogous observations could be made, of course, about "Like a Rolling Stone," another song from this period, as was demonstrated in chapter 1.

Bob Dylan's turn to specifically Christian subject matter in his work of 1979–81 led to much controversy and hand-wringing among commentators and fans, centering on issues surrounding his life and his lyrics. In terms of music, however, there was no real schism here, since gospel singing is in significant ways the sacred sister of blues singing. On the first of his gospel albums, *Slow Train Coming* (1979), Dylan's "Gonna Change My Way of Thinking" is, in every sense of the word, a blues—no less in performance than in its music and the structure of its lyrics. And "Solid Rock," on the following album, *Saved* (1980), offers as fine an example as could be desired of Dylan's use of sliding pitches, speech-song passages ("Made before the foundation"), and one-note chanting ("won't let go and I can't let go"). The opening track of *Saved* is the traditional favorite "Satisfied Mind," which showcases Dylan moaning movingly in a manner derived at least as much from country blues sources as from gospel. It is worth remembering that many of the most celebrated country blues artists, Blind Lemon Jefferson and Bukka White among them, recorded both religious and secular material, without feeling any need to adapt their basic performance approach to accommodate different lyrical subject matter. Any listener who doubts the close kinship of Bob Dylan's gospel music with the blues is invited to compare the concluding track on *Saved*, "Are You Ready?," with the B. B. King record "Rock Me Baby," a hit in 1964: the same memorable, obsessive riff; very similar tempo; and even the four-syllable verbal hook (the title lyric, in both cases).

Much of Dylan's late-period work, beginning with the album *Time Out of Mind* (1997), reveals a near obsession with the vocal stylings, expressive nature, and lyrical and musical forms of the blues. There are songs that specifically evoke the lyrics and subject matter of old black country blues (such as "Rollin' and Tumblin'" and "The Levee's Gonna Break," both from *Modern Times*, 2006) and even one from 2001 with a title that name-checks a legendary exponent of that genre ("High Water (for Charley Patton)," from *"Love and Theft,"* 2001). The very recent "Goodbye Jimmy Reed" (from *Rough and Rowdy Ways*, 2020), in turn name-checks the celebrated electric blues performer best known for the 1961 hits "Big Boss Man" and "Bright Lights, Big City"; like Dylan himself, Reed was a singer, guitarist, harmonica player, and songwriter. "My Wife's Home Town" (from the 2009 album *Together through Life*), borrows music, formal structure, and even its basic riff from the 1954 Muddy Waters record "I Just Want to Make Love to You," composed by blues master Willie Dixon (who receives a cowriting credit on the Dylan album). *Together through Life* also includes "Shake Shake Mama," which owes not a little to the 1962 John Lee Hooker blues hit "Boom Boom." The final track on *Time Out of Mind*, "Highlands," was by far the longest recorded song on any Dylan album up to that point (over sixteen minutes), and it is a blues throughout in terms of both musical form and vocal performance.

Bob Dylan, Rocker

Bob Dylan's embrace of electric instruments and drums, in his albums and performances beginning in 1965, sent shock waves through the folk-music community. At the time, many felt as if the spirit of Woody Guthrie and Pete Seeger had been betrayed. But anyone aware of Dylan's deep involvement with the blues shouldn't have been surprised in the least. Electric blues had been appearing frequently on records since the late 1940s. Dylan certainly was aware of blues artists like Muddy Waters and Howlin' Wolf, who had discovered that amplification was desirable and even necessary when their performance venues shifted from the rural South to noisy Chicago clubs. (The route north that was traveled by the country blues and many of its performers is directly noted in the title of Dylan's first fully electric album, *Highway 61 Revisited*.) In what seemed an isolated instance at the time, Dylan himself had even employed a band with drums in his arrangement of the traditional number "Corrina, Corrina" back on *The Freewheelin' Bob Dylan* album. And early in his career he recorded a wild rockabilly song of his own with a band, "Mixed-Up Confusion," released into obscurity as a 45-rpm single in late 1962. (A version of "Mixed-Up Confusion" is included on the career-spanning set *Biograph*, released in 1985.) In any case, we have seen that Dylan was already a proto-rocker at the time of his first album. His increasing engagement with blues-derived vocal techniques, reflected in his three albums from 1963 and 1964, fully prepared him to inaugurate the role of rock shouter with an electric band.

In his singing, all he needed to do was to ramp up the volume. He had already shown he could do this on certain acoustic tracks, ranging from "Highway 51" on his debut album to "It Ain't Me, Babe," the song that concludes *Another Side of Bob Dylan* (1964), with its raucous "No, no, no"s. In addition to "It Ain't Me, Babe," there are two songs on *Another Side of Bob Dylan* that reveal the singer's shouting upper register: "Spanish Harlem

Incident" and "I Don't Believe You," also known as "She Acts Like We Never Have Met." ("I Don't Believe You" was readily incorporated into Dylan's electric repertoire when he embarked on extensive touring with a band during the late months of 1965 and the first half of 1966.) The opening track of his immediately following album, "Subterranean Homesick Blues" on *Bringing It All Back Home*, showcases Bob Dylan as a defiant, unapologetic rocker—but those who had listened attentively to earlier Dylan should have known that he had always had it in him.

Side one of the LP *Bringing It All Back Home*, the electric side, is performed with a band, and the hardest rockers on it are "Subterranean Homesick Blues," "Maggie's Farm," "Outlaw Blues," "On the Road Again," and "Bob Dylan's 115th Dream." The remaining two songs are the gentler "She Belongs to Me" and "Love Minus Zero/No Limit," with softer guitars and less prominent percussion. These two are also the only songs on the entire album that might be classified as personal love songs, but they belong to that category only if we grant that Bob Dylan love songs can be very personal indeed, to the point of being idiosyncratic in lyrical and emotional content.

Dylan's vocals for all of the hard rockers on side one of *Bringing It All Back Home* are centered on single-note chanting, to a degree that could be considered exceptional even for him. "Subterranean Homesick Blues" is so preoccupied with one sole pitch that it has been called a proto-rap song, long before the fact; the song also points back, however, to the work of 1950s rock 'n' roll godfather Chuck Berry, whom Dylan himself mentions frequently as a crucial influence. (Chuck Berry's 1956 recording "Too Much Monkey Business" is often cited as an obvious forebear of "Subterranean Homesick Blues.") But there is method to Dylan's one-note chanting. Focusing on one pitch for extended periods enabled Dylan, in this early rocker phase, to concentrate on projecting his voice, paying attention to the desired level of intensity and an intentionally harsh color, without the distraction of melodic movement. This focuses the listener as well: on decibels, timbre, and rhythm. Bob Dylan was certainly capable of being a conventionally tuneful singer and songwriter, as will be seen, but this ability was totally beside the point when it came to conveying appropriately the dark worldview of "Subterranean Homesick Blues," the personal anger of "Maggie's Farm," or the surrealistic, satiric visions of "Bob Dylan's 115th Dream."

With few exceptions, Dylan's standard procedure since the mid-1960s has involved the employment of a band, whether recording in a studio or performing live. And with that, his rocker shout became part of his standard vocal equipment. It is heard again prominently on such 1970s tracks as "Idiot Wind" (*Blood on the Tracks*, 1975) and "Hurricane" (*Desire*, 1976), and later on both "Man of Peace" and "Union Sundown" from *Infidels* (1983). These selections are representative of what could easily become an extensive list. As late as 2006, Dylan unleashed his rocker voice, its volume somewhat curtailed by age but its power undiminished, on "Rollin' and Tumblin'" from *Modern Times*. Dylan's initial rocker phase was interrupted by his 1966 motorcycle accident, however, and then by a subsequent group of recordings that struck out in further new—and unanticipated—directions.

Bob Dylan, Crooner?

Bob Dylan's most surprising album of the 1960s was, paradoxically, his most conventional one: *Nashville Skyline* (1969). It is most surprising *because* it is conventional—but it is conventional by the standards of contemporary country music, a genre that at the time seemed to lie at an immeasurable distance from contemporary folk, blues, and rock music. All Dylan's preceding albums had posed conspicuous challenges for his listeners, whether of singing style, lyric content, song length, choice of instruments, or all these together. *Nashville Skyline* posed the same challenges, but only in relation to Dylan's own earlier work. To a country music fan in 1969, one unburdened by expectations about Bob Dylan, the album would likely have seemed unproblematic, the laudable effort of a "new" talent working skillfully within the genre. To a Bob Dylan fan at the same time, the great challenge was to accept *Nashville Skyline* as a *Bob Dylan* album.

What typified the country music genre of 1969? In terms of songwriting: conventional subject matter of love and loss; tracks of radio-friendly length (under four minutes, preferably closer to three); readily singable, "tuneful," major-key vocal lines; and familiar four-section popular song forms (three identical or very similar musical sections, with the second and third separated by a contrasting bridge section, a form commonly represented as A-A-B-A). In terms of instrumental performance: a generally smooth approach to rhythm, employing bass and drums, but not too prominently. The prominent instruments would be guitars, generally acoustic, except for the pedal steel guitar—an important marker of the country sound, not featured in other genres—and perhaps some piano. Last, but important, a crooning vocal style. There were significant exceptions, naturally; an entire genre can never be reduced to a set of simple formulas. But these were the conventions of mainstream "countrypolitan," Nashville-based music in the late 1960s.

Nashville Skyline respected all these conventions. But it was of course Dylan's crooning that represented the greatest shock to his established fans. Where did this new vocal mask come from? Dylan as folk troubadour in the mold of Guthrie, Dylan as bluesman, Dylan as rocker—may all be seen as interrelated musical personas in certain ways, one growing out of the other. But crooning would seem to be at the opposite pole from any and all of them. In crooning, vowels are round and long; consonants are deemphasized, plosives suppressed; vocal phrases flow within and move smoothly one to the next, avoiding unexpected rhythmic breaks. Crooning is about soothing surfaces, steering away from the abrupt, the jagged, the sudden accent—in effect, it's Peter, Paul, and Mary's "Blowin' in the Wind" as opposed to Dylan's own performance of that classic. How surprising, then, to see Dylan embracing a vocal style that would previously have seemed the antithesis of his own aesthetic.

Dylan's early and enduring admiration for country singer-songwriter Hank Williams is well documented, but Williams's influence as a singer is hardly present on *Nashville Skyline*. Williams, who died in 1953, was the embodiment of the honky-tonk style and had a rurally inflected, sometimes rough-edged singing voice. The honky-tonk influence was not absent from country music of the late 1960s, but it was by no means the predominant sound. Dylan's vocals on *Nashville Skyline* are closer to Eddy Arnold, Jim Reeves, and Glen Campbell than they are to Hank Williams—or even to Johnny Cash, who sings a duet with Dylan on the opening track, "Girl from the North Country" (the one song on the album that was not new). Nevertheless, the crooning approach surely suited the new material of *Nashville Skyline*. And Dylan's audience would have to accustom itself to the reality of Bob Dylan as a constant shape-shifter, a restless, ever-evolving artist, constantly in motion.

It would be an exaggeration to claim that there are no traces of Dylan's earlier characteristics in his singing on *Nashville Skyline*. In particular, syncopation is found throughout his vocal lines, even in "One More Night," which may be the song with the most traditional country atmosphere of all, with its lyrical melody, its theme of lost love, and its images centered on "that dark and rolling sky." The vocal syncopation is more obvious in up-tempo numbers like "Peggy Day" and "Country Pie" and in the album's hit "Lay, Lady, Lay," but in these it still lacks the edge and aggressive impact familiar from Dylan's previous work, with their marked change in his vocal color, softer dynamic level, and suppression of marked accents. Continuities from one point to another in the evolution of Dylan's singing voices may naturally be found, especially if one is determined to look for them, despite the significant changes all along the trajectory of his career. And this uncovers an important fact: that Dylan's vocal evolution is essentially cumulative. Increasingly, in his work after *Nashville Skyline*, Dylan employed a variety of singing styles within single albums, and even within single songs.

After *Nashville Skyline*, Dylan in 1970 released *Self Portrait*, an anomalous album almost totally composed of songs written by others and traditional selections that he arranged for his own performance. Crooning is abundantly in evidence on this album of covers. On his next album, *New Morning* (also 1970), Dylan croons his own amusing "Winterlude" and mixes crooning with other vocal inflections on the opening track, "If Not for You." A fine example of what might be called Dylan's composite approach to vocal styling within a single song is heard on the much later "Sweetheart Like You" from *Infidels*. This song consists of a series of musically identical stanzas, interrupted by two contrasting bridge sections. The main sections of the song are performed by Dylan in a kind of muffled croon, but in the bridge sections the suddenly violent imagery ("You can be known as the most beautiful woman/Who ever crawled across cut glass to make a deal") leads him to employ his rocker shout, to great effect. Since the rocker voice is heard only in the bridge sections, Dylan's alternation of styles also serves to articulate the musical form of the song.

For the most part, crooning in its pure state tends to recede in prominence within Dylan's vocal arsenal from the mid-1970s through the end of the century, apart from resurfacing just in parts of certain songs. Crooning makes a remarkable, late, and large resurgence, however, in his work of the 2000s and 2010s.

Dylan's rather grizzled late crooning voice is utilized to touching effect on songs like "Bye and Bye," "Floater (Too Much to Ask)," and "Moonlight" (all from *"Love and Theft,"* 2001); on "Spirit on the Water," "When the Deal Goes Down," and "Beyond the Horizon" (all from *Modern Times*, 2006); and on "Life Is Hard" (from *Together through Life*, 2009). "Beyond the Horizon" is especially notable, in that the song is clearly modeled on the 1935 Bing Crosby hit "Red Sails in the Sunset" and indicates Dylan's interest in the popular song repertoire of the 1930s and in the crooning style of singing with which it is closely linked. This apparently new interest on his part flourished some years later with the release of three albums devoted to Dylan's interpretations of old pop standards (*Shadows in the Night*, 2015; *Fallen Angels*, 2016; *Triplicate* (a three-disc set, 2017). These albums took Dylan, now in his seventies, into yet another genre not previously or remotely associated with him and revealed a new idol and model for him: Frank Sinatra! (*Self Portrait* had included Dylan's performance of the Rodgers and Hart classic "Blue Moon," but it proved an anomalous instance in terms of both the album itself and in terms of Dylan's recording career for decades following.) Challenging his dedicated listeners once again with unanticipated conventionality, Dylan remains to this day an unending source of surprises.

A Wide Palette of Vocal Colors

There are many Bob Dylan albums that could be chosen to illustrate the impressive range of singing voices and techniques he had at his disposal from the mid-1970s onward. I will briefly consider the highly regarded and well-known *Blood on the Tracks* from 1975. What follows here will by no means represent a comprehensive treatment—if such a thing could even be attempted—of Dylan's vocal strategies on this album. I offer simply a suggestion of the approaches a listener might take to initiate an appreciation of the riches presented by Dylan's voice on this album—and by extension, on many of his other albums.

Describing singing in a manner both reasonably specific and widely accessible involves a complex verbal juggling act, and overinvolvement in details will not necessarily help. One need have no specialized knowledge of vocal technique to experience the expressive impact of Dylan's singing, however, any more than one requires a knowledge of arcane wine terminology to thoroughly appreciate a glass of fine vintage. From *Blood on the Tracks*, "Simple Twist of Fate" and "Idiot Wind" are two deeply affecting songs of vastly different emotional import. Each in its own way serves to illuminate the depths, and the complexity, of Dylan's vocal artistry; while taken together, they reflect the breadth of his capabilities.

The opening stanza of "Simple Twist of Fate" demonstrates quickly Dylan's employment of two contrasting voices. He begins with something like a gentle croon, describing the scene of a couple at evening in the park. Then, toward the end of the first stanza, there is an abrupt intensifying, as he rises in volume along with pitch to a climactic rock shout on the high note and crucial word ("wished that he'd gone *straight*"), followed by an equally abrupt return to gentleness. A casual listener would note an analogous scheme characterizing the five additional stanzas. But closer attention reveals that neither the gentle croon nor the analogous scheme descriptions do adequate justice to Dylan's performance.

To explore more carefully the vocal style with which Dylan begins the song, it is necessary to consider Dylan as the song composer as well as the singer—a requirement in many cases, since he writes for himself. When Dylan introduced himself on record as a crooner with *Nashville Skyline*, it was with songs designed to underline and flatter the particular virtues of that vocal style. "One More Night" opens with long notes on the first two title words, allowing the vowel sounds to resonate as these lyrics are crooned with a wide, open mouth. The vocal line proceeds, employing many open vowel sounds. The alliterative title lyrics of "Lay, Lady, Lay" serve the crooning voice in an analogous fashion. When we turn to the opening lyrics of "Simple Twist of Fate," however, they would not seem to invite a crooning approach: "They sat together in the park." Even more significant is the musical setting of these and the following two lines of lyrics, which center almost uninterruptedly on the same single note, in a manner that would suggest instead a typical Dylan blues orientation for the singing. Dylan's choice to croon these lyrics would appear, from this standpoint, counterintuitive. On the other hand, the rhyming words on high notes in each stanza of "Simple Twist of Fate," with their long *a* vowels—straight, freight, gate, and so forth—would actually, in themselves, be well served by crooning; Dylan's hard-edged shout on these lyrics might also seem a contrarian vocal gesture.

What is going on? The mismatch of vocal style with lyrics and melodic shape in "Simple Twist of Fate" is Dylan's way of adding a significant layer of meaning to his singing of this story. The uneasy fit of the opening croon represents a strategy: as listeners, we might want this emerging tale of two people to be romantic and satisfactorily rounded (like crooning itself), but something is subtly amiss from the start. And in this context, Dylan's voice on *straight* comes across like a raw howl; the man in the story feels "alone" just when he might be hoping for connection, and it is the ghost of his past ("wished that he'd gone straight"), haunting him, that stymies the connection. No wonder that the word *straight*, preparing a rhyme with "simple twist of *fate*," needs to be projected with such painful intensity.

As the song continues, Dylan introduces variants to the singing pattern introduced in the first stanza. In the second stanza, his crooning breaks into near-speech for the description of the couple as "a little confused." In the critical fourth stanza, where the man awakes to find the room bare and the woman gone, Dylan quickly raises the volume of his voice, and it becomes speech-like for a good part of the stanza. And in the concluding stanza, notice the touching way Dylan reduces the volume of his already soft crooning on the phrase "to know and feel *too much within*"—as if literally depicting in sound the turning inward—and then allows himself another, final instance of musical onomatopoeia as he "twists" the pitch on "*twist* of fate."

The citation of these details merely skims the surface of an intricately conceived and passionately executed performance. "Simple Twist of Fate" is one of Bob Dylan's obviously masterful songs, from the standpoint of composition as well as performance, and there will be reason to return to it in subsequent chapters.

"Idiot Wind," from the same album, is like the polar opposite of "Simple Twist of Fate," angry and hectoring where the latter is basically delicate and regretful. And just as "Simple Twist of Fate" departs from delicacy at important moments, with a marked change in Dylan's singing voice, "Idiot Wind" offers moments of relief from Dylan's prevalent rock shout to mark significant turns in the lyrics and, in so doing, to create a richer, more varied listening experience. It will suffice here to call attention to a few representative examples of this procedure in "Idiot Wind."

The rather complex form of "Idiot Wind" consists of a pattern heard four times, incorporating two musically identical stanzas followed by a chorus-like part that is introduced with the title lyrics. It is at the ends of the stanzas that Dylan alters his singing voice, but it is important to note that he does not do it the same way each time, so it does not become predictable. Concluding the first stanza, Dylan simply reduces his volume on "I can't help it if I'm lucky" (as if slightly abashed to admit it). But at the end of the second stanza, Dylan virtually croons "sweet lady," elongating the already long vowel sound on *sweet* while sliding the pitch, thus underlining the irony of the expression in the context of this bitter song. Subsequently, it begins to seem as if Dylan will be content simply to lower his volume at the ends of stanzas, but later, as he sings "the springtime turned *slowly* into autumn," he returns to the voice of "sweet lady," stretching *slowly* even more—musical onomatopoeia again, emphasizing the pain of this turn of season (and this turn in the relationship). To conclude the final stanza, before the last chorus, Dylan draws out the word *sorry* to emphasize that, for all his bitterness, he also feels remorse. It must again be stressed that these observations represent just the starting point for a consideration of a skillfully crafted performance, one that will reward much repeated listening and contemplation.

While "Simple Twist of Fate" and "Idiot Wind" reveal Dylan employing his familiar voices to create unfamiliar and striking effects, other performances on *Blood on the Tracks* reveal unfamiliar voices, something unusual for Dylan at this stage of his career. Indeed, some listeners hearing "Meet Me in the Morning" for the first time, without identifying information, might even wonder if the singer was in fact Bob Dylan. Ironically, "Meet Me in the Morning" is a very traditional blues both in its lyrical structure (brief stanzas, each beginning with two identical lines) and in its chord progressions. But where one would have expected Dylan to sing such lyrics in his typical repeated-note blues style, Dylan instead executes a much more active, leaping, angular melodic line, such that one might wonder as well whether he was in fact the composer. And Dylan the singer responds to Dylan the composer with an exaggerated vocal style unlike that employed for any of his numerous earlier blues performances.

Dylan sings "Meet Me in the Morning" in a noticeably high register, creating a sense of strain, reinforced by deliberately harsh vowel sounds and restricting his air passageway so that the potential for rounding, mellowing resonance is cut off. The distinctive and disturbing timbre is an apt color for the projection of lyrics like "little rooster crowin'" and, especially, "I struggled through barbed wire." However, there is a musical strategy operative here as well. Dylan distorts his voice so that it echoes, almost eerily, the sound of the pedal steel guitar that is such a prominent feature of the arrangement—especially in the context of *Blood on the Tracks*, where the instrument appears in no other song.

A similar pairing of unusual vocal color and striking instrumental timbre is heard on the album's closing track, and only other blues song, "Buckets of Rain." The sound of Dylan's voice here has some kinship with the strained vocal on "Meet Me in the Morning," but the effect is rather more playful than effortful, a result of the significantly lower vocal register in which "Buckets of Rain" lies. There is nevertheless a metallic edge to his voice on this track, which echoes the percussive clang of Dylan's fingerpicking on his guitar. And the fingerpicking is itself a distinctive and unusual choice for Dylan at this stage; he obviously wanted a singular sound profile to characterize the finale of his remarkably varied and personal album.

The Expressivity of Silence

There is obviously much, much more that could be said about Bob Dylan as a singer. And there are those unusual tracks on which he elects to speak rather than sing (leaving aside the "talkin' blues" on the first two albums), all of them highly individual, and each thoroughly different from the others: "I Shall Be Free No. 10" (*Another Side of Bob Dylan*), "The Ballad of Frankie Lee and Judas Priest" (*John Wesley Harding*), and "If Dogs Run Free" and "Three Angels" (both from *New Morning*). But the frequency with which this celebrated man of words elects *not* to sing at all is a profound and neglected phenomenon. Dylan's employment of his harmonica as yet another voice—a nonverbal, but singularly expressive, voice—will receive the attention it clearly demands in the following chapter. Even more neglected than the harmonica, however, is Dylan's singular use of silence itself within his vocal lines.

As an initial and straightforward example, consider "As I Went Out One Morning," from *John Wesley Harding*, with its regularly recurring, long rests in the melody line:

As I went out one morning . . . . . to breathe the air around Tom Paine's . . . . . .

Each dot in the line of words above represents a beat of silence in Dylan's vocal performance, and this pattern prevails for every sung phrase in the song. The silences envelop the song in an uncanny, uneasy atmosphere, enhanced by the skeletal musical arrangement, and they offer the listener space in which to imagine a mythic, perhaps rather barren, setting for the strange fantasy conveyed by the lyrics. It would have been a simple matter for Dylan to eliminate the extended silences, providing a more traditional phrase structure for the song, but that arguably would have been a much less effective one. (In musical terms, eliminating the silent beats would have created phrases four measures in length, as opposed to six measures in length—the unconventional pattern in "As I Went Out One Morning.")

In some of Dylan's late work, the vocal lines can be defined as much by their silences as by their sung phrases. In "Love Sick" and "Highlands" (both from *Time Out of Mind*), the regular, extended vocal pauses become deliberately oppressive, like gaping holes in the singer's experience of the world, reflecting a loneliness that seems to impede even the will to sing. But no song of Dylan's employs such silences more effectively than "What Good Am I?" from *Oh Mercy* (1989):

> What good am I . . if I'm like all the rest . . . . If I just turn away . . when I see how you're dressed . . . .

The song continues in this fashion throughout, as if the listener is privy to the singer's hesitant, guilt-stricken probing of himself, striving to formulate his agonizing questions effectively. At the ends of stanzas, even the individual words become separated by silence:

> What . good . am . I?

Reading the moving, but straightforward, lyrics of "What Good Am I?" on a page would convey nothing of the *listening* experience. It cannot be overstressed that Bob Dylan is a singing musician, a composer and performer as well as a writer of lyrics. Composers and performers understand the expressivity of, and the *need* for, silence—not least in songs, at points where the lyrics might not be the most important part of the whole. Dylan may be most celebrated for songs that assault the listener with virtually uninterrupted strings of memorable words, like "Subterranean Homesick Blues" or "Mr. Tambourine Man" (both from *Bringing It All Back Home*). Such songs are, to be sure, as effective in their own way as the silence-haunted songs just brought to attention. But they are arguably no more effective.

Bob Dylan's vocal mastery is represented not only in his understanding of what to sing and how to sing it. It is reflected also in his understanding of when to withhold his singing voice, in favor of his harmonica or—the ultimate step—in favor of complete, yet eloquent, silence.

3

HIS OTHER VOICE

Bob Dylan's Essential Harmonica

Got to play your harp until your lips bleed
—Bob Dylan, "Sweetheart Like You,"
    from *Infidels* (1983)

The "harp" to which Bob Dylan refers in the epigraph above
is the humble mouth harp, or harmonica, an instrument that has accompanied Dylan from the outset of his career. I am using *accompanied* here
in the physical, not the musical, sense. Dylan cannot accompany his own
singing on the harmonica, obviously; he must choose either to sing or to
play. And he has chosen to play with such frequency that any suggestion
of a secondary role implied by the word *accompanied* must also be resisted.

The harmonica's centrality for Dylan is evident even in the physical sense.
The iconic photographs of Dylan in performance show him wearing a harmonica holder, with the instrument itself at the ready. Such an image may
be found on the back cover of his first album. This physical arrangement
is necessary if Dylan is to have his hands free to play the guitar, but it
also attaches the harmonica to his body. Physically as well as musically, it
offers him yet another *voice*. He has employed that voice in numerous and
imaginative ways as an integral part of his musical identity.

In Dylan's work, the harmonica performs a wide range of roles. It may be used primarily as a melody instrument or employed basically to generate rhythmic excitement. These are two extremes, but Dylan also finds numerous combinations of melodic and rhythmic usage at points along this spectrum. Melodically, his harmonica may function as more or less an echo of Dylan's singing voice (as in "The Times They Are a-Changin'," from the 1964 album of the same name), but it may also break free of any sung melody as Dylan improvises a new one, in the manner of a jazz musician playing over a given sequence of chords (as in "Absolutely Sweet Marie" from the 1966 *Blonde on Blonde*). Or Dylan might choose to reduce the melodic content in order to produce a kind of rhythmic chattering, executed with rapid oscillations between pairs of adjacent notes. This effect, which harmonica players might call tremolo, or warbling, was employed by Dylan early on. It is heard frequently on his first album, and when it is used it creates a strong contrast within a song, directing the focus away from the tune and more toward forward momentum.

The harmonica fulfills a decorative, ornamental function in some Dylan songs, but it plays a major structural role in others, "singing" entire stanzas. This represents another broad spectrum of possibilities along which Dylan locates many intermediate points of interest. The instrument may even function ironically, as in "What Was It You Wanted?" from *Oh Mercy* (1989)—here, the harmonica provides teasing nonverbal answers to groups of questions in the lyrics.

Bob Dylan found obvious models for his embrace of the harmonica in rural blues and other folk traditions. Woody Guthrie played the instrument on some of his recordings. The harmonica followed Dylan when he moved from acoustic to electric guitar, and electric blues artists such as Howlin' Wolf and Little Walter were exemplary harmonica players whom he could emulate.

Dylan is not the only folk-rock performer to utilize the harmonica, as anyone familiar with Neil Young's "Heart of Gold" can attest. And Stevie Wonder was keeping the harmonica in the ears of popular music fans during the same decade when Dylan first came to prominence. Nevertheless, it may be claimed that no other living figure in popular song has made as consistent or as inventive a use of the harmonica as Bob Dylan. It is impossible to discuss this performing artist in a comprehensive way without considering this aspect of his music. Yet the harmonica has failed to receive its due in the voluminous literature about him.

Beginnings

Starting with the first song on his first album (*Bob Dylan*, 1962), Bob Dylan's harmonica takes its place as an essential element of his sound. Hindsight is always 20/20, but Dylan's employment of the harmonica on the album already demonstrates formal and expressive concepts that shaped his approach throughout his career. The first two songs on the album, different from each other in every way, provide conveniently representative examples of his varied, imaginative uses of the instrument.

For the opening number, "You're No Good," Dylan presents a performance in three sections, the first and last featuring vocals, with a sharply contrasting middle section performed on harmonica. The harmonica playing is characterized by the rhythmic chattering previously described. The second selection is the Dylan original "Talkin' New York," which opens with a melodic harmonica passage that reappears systematically throughout to round off Dylan's vocal stanzas. The harmonica provides a kind of instrumental refrain following each spoken verse.

Dylan's strategies for using the harmonica in these two songs initially seem counterintuitive. Why not have the instrument play the tune in a song like "You're No Good," which provides an evident melodic shape, and why not have the harmonica mimic rhythmic speech patterns in a talking blues number? But the questions, once articulated, answer themselves: Dylan obviously tailored his harmonica playing to maximize musical variety. Having a range of possibilities at his disposal, he employed those that achieved the greatest expressive contrast and formal impact.

In "You're No Good," the harmonica is necessary to create a three-part form enlivened by a marked central contrast. The multifaceted contrast here results from Dylan's change of voice, his fresh rhythms in the harmonica part and his pointed avoidance of the vocal melody. Continuity is provided through the guitar, which does not break the strumming patterns that accompanied the initial sung stanza. The chord progression underlying the harmonica passage, while not identical to the sequence heard in the vocal sections, maintains a close relationship with it.

In "Talkin' New York," the harmonica passages add a specifically melodic interest that is lacking elsewhere in the song. The recurrences of these melodic refrains assure both continuity and consistency in the overall musical shape of this song, while other formal elements are handled, as is characteristic of talking blues, in a much less predictable way. "You're

No Good" employs the harmonica in a free-spirited, improvisatory manner, while "Talkin' New York" utilizes the instrument in a more systematic fashion, to provide some overall sense of formal control.

Dylan plays harmonica on seven of the thirteen selections on *Bob Dylan*, and the instrument has an extensive role in all seven of those numbers. "Man of Constant Sorrow" introduces the formal arrangement that would become most characteristic of Dylan's work. Here the harmonica is used to echo his singing, performing partial or complete stanzas of the song in alternation with the vocal sections. But now it becomes necessary to pause and reconsider terminology. The word *echo*, while evocative, strongly suggests a subsidiary role for Dylan's harmonica, and this is largely inaccurate. In his performances the harmonica repeats a vocal melody *literally* only on rare occasions. Generally, it paraphrases the vocal melody as a whole or in part, which is the case with "Man of Constant Sorrow." The harmonica stanzas begin with long-held notes, paralleling the long notes that occur in the opening lines of vocal stanzas. The harmonica then proceeds to paraphrase the melodic shapes that were just sung. The pattern would seem a classic instance of the call-and-response concept that informs so many of the African American musical traditions that have had a profound influence on Bob Dylan throughout his musical life. Surely *response* serves more appropriately than *echo* to describe Dylan's actual practice in "Man of Constant Sorrow."

Procedures analogous to those heard in "Man of Constant Sorrow" characterize some other songs on *Bob Dylan* that feature the harmonica. "Pretty Peggy-O" demonstrates call and response, but it also stands out in several significant ways. The harmonica stanzas in this performance offer essentially new melodies over the chord progressions of the sung verses and synthesize these fresh melodic ideas with aggressive rhythmic chattering. The harmonica dominates the song utterly; a harmonica stanza actually precedes the vocal entrance, and the performance concludes with two additional, complete harmonica stanzas. In terms of call and response, with "Pretty Peggy-O" it therefore becomes necessary to ask which is the call, and which the response? In most songs, a safe assumption is that the human voice is the primary agent, but in this instance, Dylan's practice with the harmonica bedevils that assumption. It is obvious that his harmonica usage resists facile generalizations. No small part of Dylan's musical artistry, it is a rich and complex phenomenon, which unfortunately seems to have discouraged commentators from discussing it.

With the single exception of "Man of Constant Sorrow," the songs on *Bob Dylan* that employ the harmonica are somewhat lighter in tone than those that do not, but it would be stretching a point to posit a consistent rationale for Dylan's choices along these lines. Rather, it is apparent that whenever this performer does choose to utilize his harmonica voice, he has in mind significant and compelling ways to do so.

Three Early Classics

With his second album, *The Freewheelin' Bob Dylan* (1963), the young performer came into his own as a songwriter. The album contains at least four songs that have established themselves as Dylan classics, three of which—"Girl from the North Country," "Blowin' in the Wind," and "Don't Think Twice, It's All Right"—prominently employ the harmonica. "A Hard Rain's a-Gonna Fall" is the exception here, and while harmonica music might have provided some relief from the insistent sound of Dylan's voice, hurling apocalyptic imagery at the listener throughout this longest song on the album, such relief would seem to be exactly what Dylan wanted to avoid. The other three songs all feature the harmonica in a call-and-response pattern; typically, the response paraphrases the vocal melody. I will consider these three songs in an order that demonstrates Dylan's increasingly sophisticated development of this formal strategy. It will also become apparent that the harmonica passages in these songs, in terms of their placement and expressive characteristics, establish important relationships with Dylan's lyrics. In effect, the harmonica—Dylan's instrumental voice—is beginning to "hear" the words, not just the melody, that his human voice is singing.

Dylan's performance of "Girl from the North Country" presents four successive vocal stanzas with guitar accompaniment. The song could have ended there, since all the lyrics have been sung by that point. But just when we're convinced this will be a song without harmonica, the instrument enters and plays a complete stanza, gently paraphrasing the vocal tune. The idea of *delaying* a harmonica entrance, substantially so in this case, is one that Dylan will revisit for even greater impact in such later songs as "Chimes of Freedom" and "Desolation Row."

In "Girl from the North Country," the harmonica stanza fulfills both formal and expressive functions. It rounds off the story told by the lyrics; the single vocal stanza that remains is simply a reprise of the opening stanza. But the harmonica also contributes a deepening of emotion musically, as it enters immediately after the most intensely personal stanza of lyrics: the singer has "often prayed" that his long-lost love still remembers him. The delicate melodic curves Dylan plays on the harmonica serve as a voice for what is not (or cannot) be stated (or sung) in words. It might be said that the instrument intones the singer's silent prayer. It is very touching, and the poignancy is achieved only because Dylan withholds the harmonica prior to this point.

After the harmonica stanza, the reprise of the opening lyrics assumes a new intensity. The singer asks the listener once again to remember him to the north-country girl, perhaps because he now realizes that he may not be remembered otherwise. The harmonica then returns to present a brief conclusion, improvising on the song's basic chord sequence. Lingering at first on a pointed dissonance, as if to underline the feeling of loss and regret that underlies the song, the music resolves at last, allowing the listener—and, one presumes, the singer—to move on.

Dylan's use of the harmonica in "Blowin' in the Wind" is at once economical and brilliantly effective. After each vocal refrain ("The answer is blowin' in the wind"), Dylan's harmonica plays particularly blunt paraphrases of the "answer" melody to conclude the stanzas. The homely harmonica passages offer no comfort, as they reflect and reinforce the absence of any satisfying verbal answer.

Is there a kind of brutal punning here? The harmonica is of course "blowin'" in the singer's "wind." If the harmonica is accepted as a kind of musical metaphor, this line of thought may be pursued well beyond the surface level. Like the wind itself, the harmonica can yield no definite answer. And the instrument's melodic paraphrase of the vocal melody is skeletal and angular. To employ a performer's term, Dylan is *ghosting* the melody. As an instrumental response to the vocal refrain, it constitutes a singularly elusive "answer," as elusive in its own way as Dylan's vocal answer is to the song's persistent questions. You could sing the tune along with the harmonica music, but only if you already knew that melody well. Otherwise you'd have to search hard to find the traces of the tune in the harmonica music, just as you'd have to search hard to find the answers that are blowin' in the wind.

"Don't Think Twice, It's All Right" synthesizes the procedures employed in the two songs just discussed. Dylan's harmonica playing marks formal separations between the vocal stanzas, just as is the case with "Blowin' in the Wind." But in "Don't Think Twice, It's All Right" the harmonica also adds a full concluding stanza of its own, assuming at the end an importance that would not have been anticipated from the brevity and character of its preceding appearances. This usage recalls the late, sudden, and essential role of the instrument in "Girl from the North Country."

After each of the first three vocal stanzas in "Don't Think Twice, It's All Right," the harmonica plays passages that are not truly paraphrases, rather music that seems distinctly its own. The guitar accommodates the harmonica with chord progressions that do not correspond exactly to the progressions that previously accompanied the vocal phrases. To my ears, this harmonica music is suggestive of a train whistle, an evocation that has a long association with the harmonica. The analogy is appropriate to this song of departure, even though the singer is departing (initially, at least) on foot, because of the extensive history that train imagery has in folk ballads and blues—as a symbol of movement and freedom. ("Midnight Special" is one of many classic examples. Dylan's own specific contribution to the train-harmonica genre is "It Takes a Lot to Laugh, It Takes a Train to Cry," from the 1965 album *Highway 61 Revisited*.)

After the voice has sung its last stanza, the harmonica embarks directly on a free melodic paraphrase of an entire vocal stanza, with the guitar now supplying the expected chord patterns. The feeling of paraphrase is fresh, since Dylan has avoided it up to this point, while the harmonica also retains something of its train-whistle coloring during this purely instrumental stanza. The long instrumental conclusion underlines the verbal silence that has now settled on the failed relationship described in the preceding lyrics. The singer, having told his ex-partner "You just kinda wasted my precious time," is headed down that long, lonesome road with nothing more he can say and nothing left to comfort him but his music.

The important contribution made by the harmonica to "Don't Think Twice, It's All Right" may be gauged by listening to a demo performance of the song that Dylan recorded for his publisher, using just guitar as accompaniment. This performance is now commercially available on both volumes 7 and 9 of the so-called *Bootleg Series*, and it offers a telling contrast to the version of the song released on the *Freewheelin'* album. Despite many similarities, the latter performance achieves an added dimension of musical and emotional richness, which is due to Dylan's telling employment of his harmonica.

Continuing Evolution

In Dylan's performances of "Blowin' in the Wind" and "Don't Think Twice, It's All Right" on *The Freewheelin' Bob Dylan*, the harmonica interludes separating the vocal stanzas are all of equal duration. With the opening title song on his next album, *The Times They Are a-Changin'* (1964), Dylan chooses to experiment with this aspect of song structure by varying the length of the harmonica interludes between vocal stanzas. The first such harmonica passage is relatively short, while the last one, which sets off the crucial final stanza ("The line it is drawn, the curse it is cast"), is the longest. An analogous process informs the use of the harmonica in "Like a Rolling Stone," as we have seen in chapter 1. A particularly effective instance of Dylan adjusting the harmonica's prominence—or lack of it—as a song progresses is found in "Chimes of Freedom," from *Another Side of Bob Dylan* (1964). This song also develops the tactic of delaying the harmonica's entrance, which appeared first in "Girl from the North Country."

"Chimes of Freedom" is one of Dylan's epic songs, in terms of both length and poetic ambition. The lyrics describe feelings and images evoked by a ferocious thunderstorm, in which lightning and thunder, hammering hail and electric-light arrows, mingle to produce a synesthesia: "chimes of freedom flashing." The whirling words prioritize sound over sight, emphasizing "bells" and "tolling," so that one might have expected the harmonica to take a major part in this song. Instead, Dylan demonstrates his understanding of an artistic principle articulated much later by another great songwriter, Stephen Sondheim, namely that "less is more."

"Chimes of Freedom" consists of six long stanzas, and it is only after the fourth of these that the harmonica makes its first, abbreviated entrance— barely sufficient to register its presence, and insufficient to register as significant paraphrase or response. What suddenly awakens the harmonica at this late juncture? Perhaps, in a striking paradox, it is aroused by the first direct evocation in the lyrics of the human voice: the chimes of freedom are now "tolling for the tongues with no place to bring their thoughts." Is Dylan relaxing for a moment the rush of his own thoughts, in order to provide a place for these other tongues to be heard—those of the deaf, blind, mute, and whoever else—tongues perhaps rendered inarticulate by having "no place to bring their thoughts"? In any event, the harmonica effects a formal demarcation in the lyrics at this point, as the storm begins to abate with the next stanza. After this fifth stanza is sung, the harmonica offers its sole sustained contribution to the song, soaring to a penetrating high note as it paraphrases the vocal melody of the stanza's last two lines. It is the previously taciturn harmonica that can now bring this intensely poetic, verbally dense song to its climax, expressing deep feelings that lie beyond the scope of even Dylan's words. After this, the final stanza of "Chimes of Freedom" is sung, depicting the storm's ending and acknowledging the worth of "every hung-up person in the whole wide universe." The harmonica provides a quick concluding phrase of farewell.

Several of Dylan's best-known songs from the mid-1960s make use of a delayed harmonica entrance. Examples are "She Belongs to Me" and "Mr. Tambourine Man," both from the 1965 album *Bringing It All Back Home*. But surely his most spectacular use of this practice is heard in "Desolation Row," the truly grand finale to the album *Highway 61 Revisited*. The song proceeds without a trace of the harmonica for nine elaborate stanzas, by which time it is already longer than any other song previously recorded by Dylan, having passed the eight-and-a-half-minute mark. Without warning, the harmonica then enters to perform an entire stanza, presenting a relatively close paraphrase of the vocal melody. Dylan's voice follows with its final stanza, after which the now-liberated harmonica plays yet another complete stanza to conclude the eleven-minute song.

There is an obvious rationale for employing the harmonica to set apart the last vocal stanza. In terms of the listening experience, the instrumental stanza provides a break from the wondrous but exhausting onslaught of Dylan's words, allowing the listener some space to ponder and absorb them. But this break also helps prepare the significant shift in perspective that characterizes the concluding stanza of lyrics. It is at this point that the song's "I," who was specifically present in the lyrics only once prior to this, reappears at center stage to address a previously unacknowledged "you" (perhaps the listener?), resulting in a dramatic change of tone.

In the first stanza of "Desolation Row," "I" is casually introduced, along with his "Lady," as an observer of life in and around "Desolation Row." The following eight stanzas present what might be called an allegorical, apocalyptic phantasmagoria of contemporary life as seen through the singer's eyes. (Extravagant songs merit extravagant descriptions.) A cast of characters is introduced, ranging from Cain and Abel to Romeo and Ophelia, and from Casanova and Einstein to Ezra Pound and T. S. Eliot, and they are accompanied by others newly invented—a jealous monk, Dr. Filth, calypso singers, and many others. This all culminates in nothing less than the launching of the *Titanic*. It is then that the harmonica abruptly enters, to bring us back down to earth. Finally, in the last vocal stanza, it is just "I" and "you," and the everyday reality of a letter sent (and a broken doorknob, to add some final metaphoric resonance). The lyrics for this stanza may be interpreted as offering an explanation of what was previously presented. We are told that the "you" of the song mentions many people, presumably in the letter, all of them "quite lame," whom the singer had to reconceptualize and rename. The singer's creative process apparently resulted in the visions and stories of Desolation Row that "I" just recounted.

Wrapping things up, the singer claims "Right now I can't read too good"—wonderfully ironic, considering the exceptionally literate and literary references in the preceding stanzas—and asks for no more letters to be sent, unless they are mailed from Desolation Row. With this kiss-off, Dylan renounces any remaining interest in words and seems to invite his harmonica to finish the song. The second, final, harmonica stanza offers a concluding intensification rather than a mere repetition, performing a more elaborate paraphrase of the vocal melody with just a hint of pushing the tempo. It is an additional irony that this remarkably verbal song ends up bottom-heavy, so to speak, with harmonica music.

An objection might be raised to the preceding discussion, insofar as the presence and placement of the harmonica passages in "Desolation Row" have been justified almost completely by their relationships to Dylan's lyrics. Rather than disputing this objection, I would suggest that the song represents an extreme point on the spectrum of possible lyrics-to-harmonica relationships in Dylan's work. It has already been established that the harmonica more typically plays an important role in the articulation of musical form and the enrichment of emotional content. In any case, "Desolation Row" is an exceptional song, in Dylan's output or in anyone's output, and from virtually any point of view.

The ultimate delaying tactic for placing a harmonica passage in a song would naturally be to withhold the harmonica until the very end, after the singing has come to its conclusion, thus making the instrument's entrance a complete surprise. In such a case the challenge is to make the instrumental coda a significant addition, rather than merely an ornamental, or even a superfluous, one. Dylan offers a particularly compelling instance of meeting this challenge in his performance of "Idiot Wind" on the album *Blood on the Tracks* (1975). When the creator of the already world-famous "Blowin' in the Wind" introduced another song with "wind" in the title, one might have expected the harmonica to assume a prominent role throughout the new song. Typically, Dylan subverts such expectation. It is only when this very long song has been completely sung that the harmonica appears, with a paraphrase of the vocal line from the preceding (very long) stanzas. The harmonica playing arrives on the heels of the surprising and wrenching concluding lyrics, "We're idiots, babe/It's a wonder we can even feed ourselves." The harmonica passage fades out in midstanza, as if it might have continued right through to the end of the tune. The fade-out could even suggest that the "idiot wind" continues blowing unceasingly, an implication certainly supported by the song's lyrics.

One other striking connection of Dylan's harmonica with "wind" in a song's lyrics may be heard at the very end of the concise and cryptic "All Along the Watchtower," from the album *John Wesley Harding* (1967). The harmonica is present from the outset of this performance, but the connection is made only with the final phrase in the lyrics, which is the only time *wind* is sung ("The wind began to howl"). After this phrase, the harmonica plays a particularly intense coda, focusing on a repeated pitch and its lower neighboring note, as if underlining the words with a kind of musical onomatopoeia. This also could imply, in retrospect, that the wind represented by the harmonica has been howling from the beginning of the song.

Another very effective harmonica coda is heard in "License to Kill," from the album *Infidels* (1983). This is one more instance of Dylan withholding the harmonica until all the lyrics have been sung. The lyrics end with an open question ("Who gonna take away his license to kill?") and, in an analogy to Dylan's procedure in "Blowin' in the Wind," the harmonica then provides an "answer" that is in no real sense an answer, allowing the poignancy of the question to hang unresolved. The harmonica's belated entrance is the more affecting in light of its previous absence, particularly since the question has been sung three times previously without an instrumental response. The harmonica provides a memorable paraphrase of an entire vocal stanza, ending with the melody of "Who gonna take away his license to kill?" and the track comes to a clear musical ending, the seeming conclusion that much more sorrowful for the lack of any lyrical resolution.

In discussing Dylan's harmonica codas, I would feel remiss not to mention the exquisite, improvisatory, free-tempo conclusion of "What Can I Do for You?" (from *Saved*, 1980). Here, the harmonica is accompanied by an equally improvisatory organ, the former soaring into the high register of the latter, both instruments prolonging and intensifying the echoes of the final lyric line—again a question, the one posed in the song's title. It is the pleading yet thankful query of the sinner who has been granted salvation, a query ascending into a place beyond measured time.

More Answers Blowin' in the Wind

Bob Dylan continued to explore new approaches to the role of the harmonica as his active recording and performing career continued into its second and third decades, and beyond. Perhaps no song of Dylan's employs the harmonica in as revelatory a manner as "What Was It You Wanted?" from *Oh Mercy* (1989). Once again Dylan is playing with the concept of the harmonica "answering" questions posed in his lyrics.

From the outset, "What Was It You Wanted?" establishes an "I" and "you" relationship in the lyrics, a relationship that will characterize the entirety of the song. One might be reminded of the "I" and "you" in the concluding vocal stanza of "Desolation Row." The singing "I" immediately launches into a series of questions addressed to "you" (who? the listener?): "What was it you wanted?" and "What's going on in your show?" Then the singer, promising to "be back in a minute," allows the harmonica to enter and complete this opening stanza with a new phrase of music, while "you" presumably uses this time to "get it together" and prepare the answers to the questions that have been posed.

The following stanzas reveal that the answers never come, only more questions. But there is a different problem—one of perspective, of imagined space—already at the end of the first stanza. The singer is also the harmonica player. This means that the performer of this song never physically goes anywhere when he sings "I'll be back in a minute," he only changes voices, and this muddles considerably the identity of the song's "I." Has Dylan split himself into two alternating personas, one expressing itself vocally and the other instrumentally?

The enigma deepens as the harmonica continues to provide the concluding music for succeeding stanzas, all of which pose unanswered questions. On a surface level, the harmonica is providing nonverbal space for the listener to ponder the strings of queries, while it is simultaneously marking formal divisions in the song's structure. Much is also implied under the surface, however, with music being an ideal medium for implying as opposed to clarifying; the possible implications are many and can even be mutually contradictory. Is the harmonica actually answering the questions—which is to ask whether the harmonica is playing the part of "you" in the song? Or is it representing a refusal to answer the questions, the "you" mocking the "I"? Or does the harmonica stand in for the "I," now mocking the "you" who seems increasingly incapable of providing meaningful answers as the song goes on? Is Dylan on some level presenting an elaborate in-joke based on the idea so intimately associated with him: that the answers are "blowin' in the wind"?

Obviously, these questions are unanswerable, which almost certainly is Dylan's intent. "What Was It You Wanted?" could be interpreted simply as an elaborate tease, and indeed Dylan's lyrics play with the ambiguous listening experience set up in the song. The singer (Dylan? "I"?) taunts "you" (us? the listeners?) with "Has the record been breaking?" and "Did the needle just skip?" and hilariously, in the final stanza, with "Are they playing our song?" But serious issues are suggested as well. When the lyrics ask, "What was it you wanted when you were kissing my cheek?" and then continue with references to somebody who might have been lurking "in the shadows" when the kiss took place, they could refer to some kind of romantic triangle, but a dark analogy hinting at a biblical betrayal is perhaps more likely. In his much earlier "With God on Our Side" (from *The Times They Are a-Changin'*), Dylan specifically refers to Christ's betrayal by a kiss, so reference to this Gospel incident is a part of his songwriting history.

Conundrums and paradoxes concerning the nature of interpersonal relationships, and even of personal identity, are embedded within the tantalizing riddles of "What Was It You Wanted?" One of the most pointed questions in the lyrics, arising relatively late in the song's progress, is "Who are you anyway?" But it is the inescapable, implacable harmonica, utterly consistent in its music and seemingly oblivious to the escalating questions, that is most necessary for sustaining the song's rich ambiguities. The ultimate paradox is that the harmonica's role is essential to the very identity of a song that, largely because of the harmonica's role, itself raises many questions of identity. And the harmonica retains its musical stoicism right to the end. The final question in the lyrics (which arguably should have been the first question asked, "Are you talking to me?") is followed by reiterated variations of the harmonica's characteristic phrase. Just at the point when we are anticipating a fade-out, Dylan stops the song, and the harmonica, abruptly. There will be no answers. To employ a Dylan song title, "nothing was delivered."

Or, just maybe, something was. I have come to hear this song, at least on one level, as Dylan's own questioning of his admirers, particularly his more obsessive and demanding fans: what, after all, do you want of me? And this opens the possibility of hearing the harmonica also as Dylan himself, insisting unwaveringly: I am a musician, and I give you music, and that really should be sufficient. While eluding conclusive interpretation, "What Was It You Wanted?" remains Bob Dylan's definitive call-and-response song, at once superbly ironic and disturbingly serious.

One additional irony is worthy of note. "What Was It You Wanted?" employs a variant of blues form in the chordal and rhythmic structure of its stanzas. As a musician so well versed in the blues, Dylan is aware that blues lyrics typically offer answering phrases, or punchlines, at the conclusions of individual stanzas. Many who listen frequently to Dylan's work would be aware of this as well, if only from familiarity with Dylan's own songs in blues form. Consider this stanza of "She Belongs to Me":

> You will start out standing, proud to steal her anything she sees.
> You will start out standing, proud to steal her anything she sees.
> But you will wind up peeking through her keyhole down upon your
>   knees.

Another example is the final line of "On the Road Again" (from *Bringing It All Back Home*, 1965): "Then you ask why I don't live here. Honey, how come you don't move?" With this history as background, the harmonica's nonverbal responses at the ends of questioning blues stanzas in "What Was It You Wanted?" become enriched with yet another layer of cleverness and intensity.

In his twenty-first-century recorded work, Dylan seems for the most part to have abandoned the harmonica. One could be forgiven for assuming that this was attributable to the diminishing powers that typically accompany aging. But just when a listener might least have expected it, Dylan's harmonica makes a single and extended reappearance, as an essential part of the lovely instrumental coda to "Spirit on the Water" on *Modern Times* (2006). Can it be coincidence that this passage directly follows these final lyrics: "You think I'm over the hill/You think I'm past my prime/Let me see what you got/We can have a whoppin' good time"?

4

BOB DYLAN AS COMPOSER, I

Melody, Harmony, and Rhythm

To qualify as a composer, a performing songwriter should certainly be more than a competent tunesmith who spins out singable melodies over predictable three- or four-chord progressions accompanied by a regular beat. It is the mission of this chapter to demonstrate that Bob Dylan is indeed a great deal more than that competent tunesmith. And it is not simply the case that Dylan's melodies, harmonies, and rhythms are often of uncommon interest and expressivity, as many examples will serve to illustrate. It is, more significantly, that in Dylan's best songs the isolation of any single musical element—melody, harmony, or rhythm—ultimately proves artificial and necessitates the inclusion of other elements in order to fully articulate its function as part of an integrated musical whole. In other words, Bob Dylan—like all the greatest songwriters—*composes* the various elements of music into integrated musical structures, or *compositions*. His musical compositions function in synchrony with his lyrics to produce remarkable songs.

What is important here is to facilitate the understanding and appreciation of Dylan as a creator of *music*, in addition to words, and quite apart from his abilities as a performer of his own (and others') songs. The fact that Dylan's works have always had enormous appeal for other performers attests to their value purely as compositions, independent of Dylan's own interpretations.

With that said, it is still essential to reassert that Dylan is a performing composer, and the crucial documents are not collections of printed lyrics or musical notation; rather, they are his issued recordings and his live performances, only a tiny percentage of which are available on officially released recordings. These documents reveal that Dylan regards his compositions not as works fixed in stone, but as something closer to detailed outlines, with both music and lyrics subject to spontaneous variations and elaborations, slight or significant, during the act of performing them. This need not inhibit consideration of Bob Dylan as a composer, as long as it is always kept clearly in mind. The recordings under discussion throughout this book should be understood as particular realizations of Dylan's compositions—important realizations, to be sure, but by no means exclusive of others.

Melody and Harmony

> I wish I could write you a melody so plain,
> That could hold you, dear lady, from going insane.
> —Bob Dylan, "Tombstone Blues,"
>   from *Highway 61 Revisited* (1965)

Bob Dylan certainly could write melodies, both "plain" and unusual. You rarely hear Dylan acclaimed as a melodist. But if it's a simple matter of fashioning a memorable tune, Dylan surely can deliver the goods when he wishes. "One More Night," from *Nashville Skyline* (1969), fulfills all the traditional criteria. The melody line for the main sections of the song begins on the keynote (or tonic, "do" in the scale) and then gradually arcs higher in two succeeding brief, easily singable phrases. The second half of the line essentially reverses the process with equally brief, singable phrases, repeating the high note, then gracefully descending back to the tonic. The basic shape of the line, for all its conventionality, suits perfectly the image in the lyrics, that of the singer staring upward at the stars and moon, but feeling downcast because "tonight no light will shine" on him. The melody of the contrasting (bridge) section, beginning with "I was so mistaken," is set apart by starting on a new pitch, the highest note of all so far in the line, and descending scale-wise from there.

Yet, in terms of melody alone, Dylan reveals his particular artistry in "One More Night," by departing from convention and expressively altering the final stanza. Just when a literal repetition of previously heard words and music is anticipated, as we're hearing for the last time of the wind blowing "high above the tree," the melody line suddenly takes the singer into what is by far the highest register in the song. This provides most effective musical imagery and makes the final melodic descent that much more telling. Dylan's tender rendering of these high notes exemplifies the synergy between composer and performer in his art and exemplifies also his technical skill as a singer.

As a composer, Dylan understood well the impact of unexpected high notes in the overall shaping of a melody. In "Just Like a Woman" (from *Blonde on Blonde*, 1966), his melody line continually employs the upper tonic note for significant words—in the refrain, for every "yes, she does" and for "aches just like a woman." But at the end of the bridge section (which starts with "It was raining"), the line abruptly leaps to the next scale degree *above* the upper tonic, forcefully underlining "ain't it clear" on the highest sung notes in the song.

Another example of this type occurs in the chorus sections of "Forever Young" (referring to the slower of the two versions on *Planet Waves*, 1974). These choruses take the voice suddenly leaping into its upper register, following verses that lie considerably lower in the singer's range; the melody line as a whole spans a full two octaves, highly unusual not only for Dylan but for popular song generally. An analogous effect is created within each stanza of "Simple Twist of Fate" (from *Blood on the Tracks*, 1975), when the initially low-pitched vocal line ascends by leaps to a single high note on a crucial word: "straight," "freight," "gate," and so on—important words also because they provide rhymes for "fate." Dylan alters his vocal timbre on these high notes to underscore the expressive impact, as discussed in chapter 2.

Unexpected melodic leaps into a lower register can have an equally expressive effect. The chorus of "Forever Young" concludes with an abrupt jump from the highest register used in the song back down to the lowest, ending in fact with the lowest note heard in the melody line. In his performance of this song on *Planet Waves*, Dylan strains for this note; the effect is curious, and touching. In "Where Teardrops Fall" (from *Oh Mercy*, 1989), the vocal line falls precipitously every time the title lyrics are sung, for obvious but expressive reasons.

Melodic high notes can also prove effective when a listener is led to expect them, while being forced to wait. Nowhere is this better illustrated than in the famous chorus of Dylan's "A Hard Rain's a-Gonna Fall" (from *The Freewheelin' Bob Dylan*, 1963), on which the voice moves steadily upward on repetitions of the words "it's a hard," finally reaching the highest melody note in the song (the upper tonic), and with that allowing the phrase "it's a hard rain's a-gonna fall" to be sung complete at last, with the appropriate melodic descent at the end. However, melody alone does not fully account for the impact of this climax. Dylan's employment of harmony needs to be considered as well. When the voice initially reaches its highest pitch, the guitar does not provide the expected chord of final resolution (the tonic chord) but makes us wait yet further—for one more "it's a hard"—before the harmony reaches its goal, catching up, so to speak, with the melody.

Details of Dylan's unexpected chord choices may seem to take us into highly technical realms, but in terms of *listening*, such effects are readily heard. It is in fact a favorite compositional device of Dylan's to withhold the tonic chord when his melody line ascends to the upper tonic note. This avoids a premature feeling of completion and makes that high pitch doubly expressive. (This is the harmonic strategy employed for accompanying the melodic high notes cited previously in "Simple Twist of Fate.") Musicians will recognize that in "A Hard Rain's a-Gonna Fall," as well as in "Simple Twist of Fate," Dylan chooses the chord built on the fourth scale degree (the subdominant, or IV chord), in lieu of the tonic (the chord built on the first scale degree, or I chord) to harmonize the climax of his melodies. But musical literacy is not required to appreciate the surprise and beauty of these choices, especially within the chordal vocabulary that typifies much of Dylan's music. Harmony inescapably works its way into a consideration of Bob Dylan as a creator of melody.

Any discussion of Dylan as a melodist should include a reference to the memorable melody that constitutes the chorus of "Mr. Tambourine Man" (from *Bringing It All Back Home*, 1965). The gentle melodic curves are musically effective in themselves, and also reflect in sound the wandering, searching character of Dylan's lyrics. But here again, the chords accompanying the melody contribute an essential element to the music's expressivity, and once more it is Dylan's choice of the IV chord to harmonize the upper tonic note of the melody that proves the decisive factor. In this case, the melody of the opening chorus actually begins on that upper tonic, and the

avoidance of the expected tonic chord at that point sets the whole opening phrase harmonically askew, providing a special punch to Dylan's "Hey,
Mis-ter Tambourine Man" and introducing, by means of chord choice, the
unpredictable, wayward essence of the song. In his recorded performance,
Dylan precedes the opening chorus with a guitar introduction, strumming
the tonic chord, thus assuring that the impact of the chord change when
his voice enters will be strongly felt.

What Dylan achieves with the very traditional, limited pitch materials he
employs in "Mr. Tambourine Man" is admirable. For this is but a four-chord
song, and the melody requires only six notes of a conventional major scale.
Throughout both the choruses and the verses of "Mr. Tambourine Man,"
the melody line wanders from the upper tonic to the lower tonic. Dylan,
however, multiplies the ingenuity of harmonizing the upper tonic note with
the IV chord by harmonizing the *lower* tonic note with the IV chord as well,
at every point save one: the final note of the chorus. The song tends, for the
most part, to rotate a progression of three chords—those on the tonic (I),
subdominant (IV), and dominant (V, built on the fifth degree of the scale)—
in the pattern IV-V-I-IV (in the key of C major, that would be F major–G
major–C major–F major), instead of the standard I-IV-V-I. Consequently,
the long verses all remain in a state of continuing harmonic suspension,
never settling at all, and the choruses settle on the tonic chord only when
they conclude with Dylan singing "I'll come followin' *you*," establishing a
feeling of goal, or at least of direction, at last. (Guitarists or pianists might
experiment singing the opening phrase of the chorus, accompanying it with
a progression that substitutes I chords for the two IV chords in Dylan's pattern. The difference is striking, and reveals the wisdom of Dylan's choices.)
The harmony between the chord progressions and the song's lyric content
is perfect.

Accompanying the start of a vocal line with a chord other than the tonic
is a striking compositional choice on Dylan's part in "Mr. Tambourine Man,"
and a more extreme instance occurs in "Idiot Wind" (from *Blood on the
Tracks*). Here, there is no instrumental introduction, and the voice enters
immediately on what turns out not to be the tonic pitch (although we
can't know that yet), accompanied by a *minor* chord. It is not until the end
of the opening phrase ("stories in the press") that we hear what turns out
to be the tonic (*major*) chord in the accompaniment, and yet further time
passes before the voice actually sings what turns out to be the tonic note of

the scale. This is all a technical means of saying that it takes a while before a listener gets a clear sense of what key "Idiot Wind" is actually centered in—which in turn is a technical way of saying that, from the outset, it is a song dominated by a feeling of instability, an instability conveyed by both melody and harmony (and of course by the lyrics; there could hardly be a more unsettling opening than "Someone's got it in for me"). It is as if the song begins in midprocess, melodically and harmonically, and it takes some time for the listener to sort out the musical relationships actually governing the piece. Musically, we are thrown into the midst of a whirlwind. And how appropriate this is for a wind song that projects anger and emotional instability to an extent scarcely matched anywhere in Dylan's, or indeed anybody's, output.

The employment of unexpected minor chords within a major-key song accounts for much of the fraught musical atmosphere of "Idiot Wind." "How strange the change from major to minor" Cole Porter wrote in his song "Every Time We Say Goodbye," and Bob Dylan makes a particular point of this in the stanzas of "Simple Twist of Fate," where a major chord is followed immediately by a minor chord on the same scale degree to mark a sudden turn in the lyrics within each stanza. These minor chords occur on the fifth vocal phrases of stanzas: "'Twas then he felt alone," "He felt the heat of the night," "She dropped a coin into the cup," "Felt an emptiness inside," and so forth. The changes from major to minor can seem like visceral shudders in the musical fabric and attest to the breadth of Dylan's harmonic imagination.

One remarkable instance of Dylan's reversing this procedure comes at the very end of the dark minor-key song "Ain't Talkin'" (from *Modern Times*, 2006). After nearly nine minutes of unrelieved minor-key music, Dylan concludes the song—and the whole album—with a bright-sounding major chord on the tonic, a chord that seems to arrive out of thin air. Coming on the heels of the lyrics "Heart burnin', still yearnin'/In the last outback, at the world's end," this major chord can seem like a bitter, ironic smile: an enigmatic musical farewell, from a master of enigmas.

Bob Dylan is very aware of the special somber coloring the use of a minor key can give. His minor-key songs span the course of his career, from the early "Masters of War" (from *The Freewheelin' Bob Dylan*, 1963) to "Ain't Talkin'" and beyond. The 2012 album *Tempest* offers two substantial examples, "Scarlet Town" and "Tin Angel," as is also the case with his latest album

(*Rough and Rowdy Ways*, 2020), which includes "My Own Version of You" and "Black Rider." Within this span are such notable efforts as "Ballad of a Thin Man" (from *Highway 61 Revisited*, 1965), "All Along the Watchtower" (from *John Wesley Harding*, 1967), "Dirge" (from *Planet Waves*), "One More Cup of Coffee (Valley Below)" (from *Desire*, 1976), "Señor (Tales of Yankee Power)" (from *Street Legal*, 1978), "I and I" (from *Infidels*, 1983), and "Man in the Long Black Coat" (from *Oh Mercy*, 1989).

Dylan's use of unexpected chord choices can occasionally go beyond matters of major and minor. No song of his utilizes a wider range of unanticipated chords than "In the Garden" (from *Saved*, 1980). Each of the five identically structured stanzas of "In the Garden" is six lines long: four identical questions form the first two and last two lines, with different material in lines three and four. Read on a page, this format would appear to be a recipe for tedious repetition, but Dylan the composer once again proves to be the essential colleague of Dylan the lyricist. Each restatement of a question within a stanza is greeted by a startling harmonic change; the second line of the stanza jolts us so far out of key as to render further expectation virtually pointless, and in fact the opening key does not return until the final line of the stanza. Only the middle (third and fourth) lines of the stanza remain relatively stable harmonically. And no listener needs to consult a music textbook to hear the steady, striking rise in the harmony from line four to line five to line six. This compositional strategy assures that, within each stanza, the reiterated questions will be attention-demanding intensifications, not rote repetitions, in order to reflect the unparalleled importance of such questions: "When they came for Him in the garden, did they know?" "When He spoke to them in the city, did they hear?" and so forth.

Another important resource in Dylan's harmonic vocabulary is the descending bass line. This can be especially effective, and is readily heard, when it occurs against relatively static passages of vocal melody, as in the extensive chant-like sections of "It's Alright, Ma (I'm Only Bleeding)" (from *Bringing It All Back Home*), and in so many of the phrases composing "My Own Version of You" (from *Rough and Rowdy Ways*). A descending bass line is also prominent at the beginnings of stanzas in "Ballad of a Thin Man," "Lay, Lady, Lay" (from *Nashville Skyline*), "Something There Is About You" (from *Planet Waves*), and "One More Cup of Coffee (Valley Below)." In these and other such cases, the bass line provides a sense of active movement, and sometimes—particularly in minor-key songs—of restlessness. This is especially the case in "My Own Version of You," which presents the singer as a contemporary Doctor Frankenstein, attempting to conjure out of the widest-ranging lyrics and the most obsessively limited musical materials a "creature," a "creation," that will satisfy and save him. The pervasive descending bass figure here gets interrupted, systematically and effectively, by individual phrases featuring *ascending* chords, and by phrases repeating the same unstable chord whenever "bring someone to life" is sung—only to have the music fall back to its original, unadorned condition. Evoking in various ways both movement and stasis, softly played yet darkly colored and seemingly sinister in its repetitive patterns, the instrumental music in "My Own Version of You" offers an effective counterpart to the alternating expressions of ambition, determination, and frustration in the song's lyrics.

In "The Wicked Messenger" (from *John Wesley Harding*), the sparse instrumentation pushes the relentlessly moving, continually descending bass line to the forefront of a listener's awareness, giving the song a distinctive and uneasy musical character. Together with the restricted five-pitch, minor-inflected vocal melody and the oscillations between minor and major in the accompanying guitar chords, the bass line in "The Wicked Messenger" paints a musical portrait of a disturbing individual in a disturbing situation. Musically and lyrically, here is another of Bob Dylan's provocative enigmas.

"Simple Twist of Fate" also features a descending bass line, in this case at the beginning of each stanza, while the vocal line remains relatively static. Then the sung melody becomes more active (in the first stanza, on the words "tingle to his bones"), as the underlying chords present the expressive major-to-minor switch described earlier. What follows is the sudden vocal ascent to the high tonic note, which is accompanied by a nontonic chord, as cited previously in this chapter. Finally, the melody comes to rest on a low tonic note, accompanied by the expected tonic chord, to mark the ends of stanzas. In effect, "Simple Twist of Fate" provides all by itself an overview of many of the significant compositional techniques employed by Bob Dylan to enrich the melody and harmony in his work.

Dylan's range as a song composer runs from a catchy little three-chord tune like "Man Gave Names to All the Animals" (from *Slow Train Coming*, 1979), suitable for a children's Sunday-school class, to effective adaptations of preexisting melodies, to complex and uniquely personal creations like "Simple Twist of Fate." His adaptations themselves range from "Blowin' in the Wind" (from *The Freewheelin' Bob Dylan*), inspired by "No More Auction Block," to "Beyond the Horizon" (from *Modern Times*), based on "Red Sails in the Sunset." In "Blowin' in the Wind," Dylan altered the melody line of his source to assure that none of the questions in his new lyrics would end on a tonic note and that the vocal line would come to a complete rest only on "the answer is blowin' in the *wind*." With "Beyond the Horizon," Dylan altered the *rhythmic* placement of his borrowed melody line to reflect in sound the active yearning expressed in his lyrics. And here we arrive, inevitably, at the inescapable role of rhythm in shaping any melody and in the comprehensive shaping of all songs.

Rhythm

> Feel the pulse and vibration and the rumbling force.
> —Bob Dylan, "Man in the Long Black Coat,"
>   from *Oh Mercy* (1989)

Bob Dylan's slashing, staccato vocal throughout "Man in the Long Black Coat" is indeed a "rumbling force" of "pulse and vibration," serving to remind us of the extent to which the human voice can serve as a rhythmic percussion instrument. The essential element of rhythm was, deliberately, sidelined during the preceding discussion of melody and harmony (as is so often the case in musical discourse). While allowing the focus to center on pitch construction, such sidelining constitutes an artificiality that may easily give rise to a complete misconception. There can be no melody without rhythm, for it is rhythm that positions melodic pitches in time and duration. Nor can there be any sense of harmonic movement—of chord progressions and interrelationships—without rhythm.

There can, however, be rhythm independent of melody and harmony. A compelling drum solo demonstrates how musically self-sufficient rhythm can be. In our age, when rap is flourishing, perhaps the time has come for a reconceptualization of vocal melody itself: a new definition that prioritizes rhythm and leaves specific pitch content optional. It would then follow that Bob Dylan's many chant-like songs that center partially, or even mostly, on a single pitch should be included in a discussion of his approaches to composing melody. This in turn would open the doors to a deepened appreciation of vocal melody in the blues sources for Dylan's style, and in much related music. (That could provide the basis for another entire book.)

Dylan's rhythmic articulation of repeated-note phrases in "Like a Rolling Stone" was discussed previously in chapter 1. The track that follows "Like a Rolling Stone" on the *Highway 61 Revisited* album, "Tombstone Blues," has verses that are essentially spoken in rhythm by Dylan, followed by choruses ("Mama's in the factory") that are sung. In these verses, the timing and accentuation account for everything. Returning to the lyrics quoted at the beginning of this chapter's section on melody, the effect of Dylan's recorded interpretation might be represented like this, with strong accents indicated by italics:

> *I —— wish* I could *write* you a melody soplain
> That could *hold* you dear *lady*   from goinginsane
> That could *ease* you and *cool* you   and ceasethepain
> Of your *use*less and *point*less *knowledge*.

Dylan's use of timing and accents to maximize the impact of his lyrics is masterful. Notice the momentary holding back after "hold you dear lady," followed by the collapse of "going insane" into one word. These details reveal once again the synergetic relationship between composition and performance for Bob Dylan. And how appropriate that in performance Dylan's melody "so plain" is one that is reduced to the single essential element of any melody: rhythm. (The printed music for "Tombstone Blues" in *The Definitive Bob Dylan Songbook* offers a very basic vocal melody for the verses, which seems to represent a case of wishful thinking on the part of the transcriber.)

Among many other instances of Dylan's rhythmic inspiration when timing his lyrics in performance, one that is especially apposite to this discussion is found in "Stuck Inside of Mobile with the Memphis Blues Again" (from *Blonde on Blonde*). This is another song in which Dylan speak-sings many of the verses. And at the end of the seventh verse, he actually plays with the vocal rhythm in order to articulate his own loss of rhythmic impetus:

I have no   sense of   *time*.

The musical onomatopoeia is delicious. Dylan can even use the idea of time ironically. In "Handy Dandy" (from *Under the Red Sky*, 1990), the title character's rushed question "How much time I got?" is answered in even greater haste by "You got all the time in the world"; the entire exchange is squeezed with deliberate awkwardness into a rhythmic space much too limited to accommodate it appropriately. This little-known song, from a relatively obscure album, offers many instances of inspired rhythmic play on Dylan's part.

The importance of rhythm in Bob Dylan's art is reflected not only in details. Rhythm can inform the conception of entire songs. Dylan provides a fine illustration by including two radically different versions of the same song, "Forever Young," on his *Planet Waves* album. Side one of the original LP concludes with a very slow-paced interpretation that turns "Forever Young" into a lullaby. This version of the song, discussed earlier in this chapter, provides ample rhythmic space for a wide-ranging melody line and for an expressive, leisurely descending bass line at the beginnings of verses. Side two of *Planet Waves* starts out with a rocking "Forever Young" that moves much more rapidly and lasts little more than half as long. At this tempo, there is no room for the melodic intricacies of the slow version, and the soaring chorus section of the latter is nowhere to be heard. The bass line and harmonies are also different. That is to say, rhythm changes everything. One could claim that these two performances are recordings of two different songs that happen to share the same lyrics.

It is important to remember that the long-playing record format gave recording artists considerable control in ordering the listener's experience. The positioning of the two versions of "Forever Young" on the original *Planet Waves* LP suggests a prioritization of the slow version and the experiencing of the other as an alternative rendition. (A listener might have wondered whether perhaps Dylan wished to show that his tender lullaby could also serve as a bouncy play-song, lest the accusation of sentimentality be leveled at him.) The published sheet music in *The Definitive Bob Dylan Songbook* documents the slow version only. And the only live performance of "Forever Young" on any officially released Dylan album, found on *Bob Dylan at Budokan* (1978), also presents that version, which over time seems to have assumed a position as definitive.

But there is a curious twist to this history. Recording studio data indicates that the up-tempo "Forever Young," lacking a chorus section, was in fact the *earlier* form of the song, and that its metamorphosis into a lullaby was an inspired late-stage development during the actual recording sessions for the *Planet Waves* album. The Bob Dylan compilation *Biograph* (1985) includes an acoustic version of this earlier "Forever Young," recorded (for demonstration and copyright purposes at the time, rather than for official release) several months prior to the sessions for *Planet Waves*. This history reveals that Bob Dylan is a song composer deeply interested in, and committed to, compositional *process*, an artist for whom many, indeed any, of his pieces may be works-in-progress for some time. Dylan's continual alterations of his songs in live performances also attest to this and function as warnings against easy assumptions about definitive versions of his creations. In this respect, Dylan reveals his kinship with the blues artists he reveres, who also continually reinvented their songs, and with jazz musicians as well.

Another testament to the role of rhythm in conceptualizing a song, and in transforming a song in progress, is offered by the now-available recording of a preliminary rehearsal for "Like a Rolling Stone," in which the song is tried out as a *waltz*. This fragment may be found on *The Bootleg Series*, vol. 12, *The Best of the Cutting Edge*, released in 2015 (disc 1, track 14). Perhaps Dylan felt for that moment that a graceful waltz could work with the fairy-tale evocation of the opening lyrics ("Once upon a time") and then function ironically as his bitter story unfolds? Anyone who knows the finished version, however, will realize the awkwardness of the earlier attempt. The lyrics do not fit well in a triple-time setting, and in the rehearsal Dylan apparently stopped after singing just one stanza of the song.

Although Dylan employed triple meter frequently in his early songs and in his solo recordings of them, it is encountered much less often in the work he did with bands. The standard rhythmic approach in rock and electric blues utilizes a steady meter of four beats, with a strong back beat supplied by the drums on the second and fourth pulses, and this approach was readily embraced by Dylan and his accompanying instrumentalists. It is heard prominently in the released version of "Like a Rolling Stone" and in every other track on *Highway 61 Revisited* where drums are present—on this album, only "Desolation Row" is performed without percussion. Apart from "Like a Rolling Stone," the back beats are particularly marked in "Just Like Tom Thumb's Blues," where their steady punches present a fine foil to Dylan's vocal, with its exceptionally flexible rhythms.

There seems to be no special significance to Dylan's choice of triple meter for such celebrated early-career songs as "Masters of War," "A Hard Rain's a-Gonna Fall" (both from *The Freewheelin' Bob Dylan*), "The Times They Are a-Changin','" and "With God on Our Side" (both from *The Times They Are a-Changin'*, 1964), but it is important to realize that there is nothing like an oom-pa-pa waltz among them. Instead, the rhythm is marked by the guitar strumming steady, strong beats—more pa-pa-pa than anything else—while the vocal melody articulates the accents, and the guitar provides the chord changes, that define the three-beat pattern. Indeed, nothing suggesting the ballroom waltz, that decidedly bourgeois, old-fashioned dance, could be musically appropriate for songs like those cited, which proclaim their 1960s contemporaneity in decisive and even harsh terms. And this steely approach toward performing triple rhythms proved a good model for those less common occasions when Dylan would choose such a metrical orientation for songs he recorded with bands.

A good example of this is "Isis" (from *Desire*). Here, Dylan's piano substitutes for guitar, striking chords on every beat. Meanwhile, the drum accents heavily the first beat of every *other* three-beat measure—*pa-pa-pa, PA-pa-pa, pa-pa-pa, PA-pa-pa*, and so on—providing an effective rhythmic analogy for the back beat within the context of a triple meter.

Waltz-like oom-pa-pas are rare in Dylan's output, but they do occur and achieve a special impact by virtue of their rarity. "Winterlude" (from *New Morning*, 1970), with lyrics alternately saccharine ("Winterlude, Winterlude, my little apple") and winking ("The snow is so cold, but our love can be bold"), comes across as a gentle parody of a sentimental waltz. More than four decades later, in the title song from *Tempest* (2012), Dylan most appropriately chooses a waltz for his depiction of the 1912 Titanic disaster, with the "lords and ladies" and "ballroom dancers" utterly unprepared for the sinking of their supposedly indestructible ship. Altogether different from either of these is "When the Deal Goes Down" (from *Modern Times*), a steel guitar-infused, quiet country waltz with deeply serious lyrics abounding in intimations of mortality ("We live and we die, we know not why/But I'll be with you when the deal goes down"). For a final example, we could return to "Man in the Long Black Coat," a kind of rarity among rarities, where the waltz rhythm is provided by the strong bass beats along with Dylan's harsh vocal accents. It is like a waltz for ghosts that reflects in music the lyrical image of the man with "a face like a mask" who is asked by the woman (who has since disappeared with him) to dance.

Much of the finest popular music engages with the tension between expected regularity—of melodic shape, of chord progressions, of formal design, and of rhythmic elements: pulse, meter, phrasing—and the creative, unanticipated introduction of irregularities. It has been shown how this tension applies to Dylan's usage of melody and harmony, and it applies no less to his treatment of rhythm. What is of immediate relevance here are the materials of musical composition. In actual performance, of course, Dylan and any accompanying musicians may freely introduce variations of the basic compositional patterns.

Naturally, it is possible to compose memorable songs that demonstrate regularity in the musical elements mentioned previously. Among Dylan's earliest and best-known songs, "Blowin' in the Wind" and "Don't Think Twice, It's All Right" (both from *The Freewheelin' Bob Dylan*) exemplify this. Rhythmically, the two songs are characterized by an unchanging meter articulated by steady pulses in the guitar part and regular phrase lengths in the vocal line. Even in Dylan's early work, however, a marked interest in rhythmic flexibility appears, on the *Freewheelin'* album with a track like "Down the Highway," and on the next album (*The Times They Are a-Changin'*) with "Restless Farewell." The latter receives a virtually improvisatory performance, with both vocal and guitar rhythms exhibiting a high degree of irregularity; the recording bears only a passing resemblance, if that, to the printed music for the song that appears in *The Definitive Bob Dylan Songbook*. Such liberties are readily possible, even invited, in a solo performance context. But the title song from *The Times They Are a-Changin'* shows Bob Dylan already working to invest his compositions themselves with inventive rhythmic content.

In "The Times They Are a-Changin'," the opening stanza establishes the irregular phrasing pattern that will be followed in all succeeding stanzas of the song. When the third vocal phrase, "And accept it that soon you'll be drenched to the bone," is heard as an exact parallel to the opening phrase ("Come gather 'round people"), the listener expects a following fourth phrase that will analogously resemble the second phrase and provide a symmetrical close to the stanza. Such a fourth phrase does in fact occur, "If your time to you is worth savin'," but instead of ending the stanza—and indeed it cannot, with the lyrics hanging in midthought—it leads to two further phrases, and only after them does the melody come to rest with the singing of the title lyrics. Rhythmically then, the stanzas in "The Times They Are a-Changin'" are six phrases long and do not correspond to the expected, common four-phrase structure with a symmetrical two-plus-two pattern. This seems musically fitting for a song with lyrics celebrating the disruption of traditions, politically and socially. It is also noteworthy that the first and third phrases of each stanza have several beats of rest following the ends of their vocal lines, which is not true for any of the other phrases; the result is irregular phrase lengths *within* the overall asymmetrical patterning of the phrases.

The ingenuity of the phrasing in "The Times They Are a-Changin'" represents a *compositional* rather than a performance-related matter, because it remains a pattern that governs the entire five-stanza song. I dwell on this in such detail because abundant examples of a similarly inventive approach to rhythmic composition appear in Dylan's work during his career, and becoming aware of them is one of the delights of listening to Bob Dylan. It was important that he develop such an approach, since, once he began performing with a band, the kind of spontaneous rhythmic freedom displayed in solo performances like "Down the Highway" and "Restless Farewell" seemed no longer a practical possibility. In a typical ensemble performance, unless rhythmic interest is written into the actual structure of a song, the song's structure will not display rhythmic interest. Dylan's compositional incorporation of rhythmic invention runs a gamut from details within phrases to the structuring of entire sections, as we have just seen to be the case with "The Times They Are a-Changin'."

Uncommon phrase structures are found with sufficient frequency in Dylan songs to warrant the statement that rhythmic irregularity is a regularly recurring feature of his compositions. It will suffice to offer a few more, particularly striking, examples.

On the printed page, "Rollin' and Tumblin'" (from *Modern Times*) exhibits an absolute regularity of *lyric* structure: classic three-line blues stanzas, in which the first two lines of each stanza are identical. However, Dylan as composer specifies that the two identical lines in the stanzas are to be differentiated *musically*, insofar as the first is extended beyond the expected length by the accompanying band (with the expected length applying to all the other lines in the song). This seemingly straightforward device is surprisingly effective, especially in a traditionally cast blues number such as this one, keeping the listener on her toes at precisely the points when she might be inclined to relax her attention, in expectation of a repeated lyric line.

In "Romance in Durango" (from *Desire*) the occurrence of phrases having an extra beat—a sort of rhythmic hiccup—is systematic and prominent, giving this Mexican cowboy tale an uneasy edge from the start, and perhaps foreshadowing musically its tragic ending. The irregularities may be heard in every chorus section on these lines (the extra beat is indicated with italics):

> Soon the horse will take us to Du-*ran*-go . . .
> Soon you will be dancing the fan-*dan*-go.

Something similar happens in "Do Right to Me Baby (Do unto Others)" (from *Slow Train Coming*), in which periodic rhythmic quirks in the verses achieve a catchy impact, focusing attention on what might seem, without the music, to be rather rote lyrics:

> Don't wanna judge nobody, don't wanna *be*
> judged, [2   3   4]
> Don't wanna touch nobody, don't wanna *be*
> touched, [2   3   4] (etc.)

The readily heard effect here is of alternating rhythmic units of five and four pulses. The chorus of this song creates a contrast, with its regular four-pulse units, but it has its own quirk: the repetition of "like you'd have them [do unto you]" prolongs the second half of the chorus, producing asymmetry with the first half.

A delightful instrumental version of the "extra beat" effect occurs in "Goodbye Jimmy Reed," from *Rough and Rowdy Ways*. In this song, the guitar solo that concludes each vocal stanza incorporates a one-beat hic-cup, postponing the arrival of the next anticipated downbeat. The systematic recurrence of this rhythmic device defines it as an element of the song's composition; it was not merely a momentary whim on the part of the guitarist.

In the rhythmic structure of "Not Dark Yet" (from *Time Out of Mind*, 1997), the phrases are all a highly unusual ten beats in length. This is due to the extended rests in the vocal part that conclude each line of lyrics. A lesser songwriter could easily have made all these phrases a conventional eight beats long (4 + 4), but Dylan's carefully measured rests add immeasur-ably to this song's expression of weary poignancy. Other songs in which systematic pauses in the vocal line create uncommon phrase patterns have received attention previously, in the concluding section of chapter 2.

The four-line verses of "Nettie Moore" (from *Modern Times*) probably represent the apex of rhythmic irregularity in Dylan's output, once again created by rests in the vocal part that in this case are much less systematic than those in "Not Dark Yet." In "Nettie Moore," the pulses in the verse sections are almost oppressively marked in the accompaniment, against which the lyric lines stand out in their highly irregular pattern of 6 + 5 + 7 + 7 pulses (although even within this pattern, Dylan syncopates his vocal performance to provide variety from verse to verse). Clearly, as the second line of lyrics tells us explicitly, "Something's out of whack!" The rhythmic angularity is relieved in the chorus sections of "Nettie Moore," as the thumping pulses cease temporarily and the vocal phrasing becomes regular. But this might represent only the peace of oblivion, for the singer tells us that "The world has gone black before my eyes."

To round off this aspect of the discussion, the long stanzas of "Black Diamond Bay" (from *Desire*) offer as rich an illustration as could be desired of Dylan's imaginative, varied phrase structure. The opening stanza establishes the elaborate pattern for all the subsequent stanzas. After two balanced opening phrases of conventional length, the two following phrases, starting with "And all the remnants of her recent past," are foreshortened. And the expectation that regularity will be restored with the concluding lines of the stanza is upended by the rhythmic drawing out of the final words, "As the last ship sails and the moon fades away/From Black Diamond Bay." The rhythmic irregularities, as would be expected with Dylan, work effectively with the lyrics. The foreshortened phrases conclude with appropriately rushed vocal rhythms on words like "scattered in the wild wind" (first stanza), "headin' for the second floor" (second stanza), and "went to grab another beer" (final stanza). And the more leisurely vocal rhythms at the ends of stanzas are mated with lyrical descriptions of the external landscape on Black Diamond Bay, creating a distancing effect. Nowhere is this distancing more telling than in the conclusion of the entire song, when the singer ends his fantastic, mock-tragic tale with a shaggy-dog shrug, emphasized by the long notes: "And I never *did plan to* go anyway/To Black Diamond Bay."

In all aspects of rhythm, just as is the case with melody and harmony, Bob Dylan is a composer for whom irregularity—the unexpected, the unconventional, the asymmetrical—is a strategy and procedure that is systematically employed, to be expected and to be enjoyed in his work. And no Dylan recording better exemplifies the unexpected, unconventional, and asymmetrical than his very recent—and (so far) longest—offering, "Murder Most Foul" (from *Rough and Rowdy Ways*). It is challenging even attempting to describe this selection, so far does it depart from the traditional norms of songwriting, and indeed from characteristic efforts by the tradition-bucking Dylan himself. One would have to go way back to solo Dylan performances like "Down the Highway" and "Restless Farewell" to find anything analogous to the sense of improvisatory spontaneity that is sustained throughout this nearly seventeen-minute work. Yet the ambience is achieved not by Dylan performing solo, but with a backing instrumental ensemble that prominently includes piano, bowed string instruments, and percussion. These players give the impression of responding to Dylan's utterly fluid, virtually unmetered vocals as if they were one instrument, and that instrument one being played by Dylan himself—like an ensemble reading his mind as he goes along. The chordal vocabulary is, of necessity, simple, but the chord changes sound as spontaneous as Dylan's rhythmic phrasing and melodic shaping. The effect is paradoxical, seemingly inimical to the basic concept of band performances, excepting those by seasoned improvisers who have worked together for a long time.

The distinctive music of "Murder Most Foul" is totally appropriate for lyrics that seem every bit as improvised and spontaneous, for Dylan appears to range through the politics and culture of America in the 1960s (and far back and beyond) in a free-association, stream-of-consciousness process. Of course, this effect may belie very real artistry exercised to produce it, just as might be said about the music. Dylan's vocal performance merges speech-like intoning, single-note chanting, and singing, one into another, until all boundaries are blurred. With the remarkably sympathetic assistance of his accompanying musicians, he lures the sympathetic listener into a semihypnotic state, in which the sense of time becomes suspended for both performers and auditors.

"Murder Most Foul" is the creation of a consummate songwriter. On the other hand, it could also be seen as an attempt to create a kind of primordial song, a work in which both lyrics and music evade the systematic, organizing principles of form that are traditionally associated with songwriting. Even from the most basic formal standpoint, dividing the selection into traditional stanzas and sections is an arbitrary enterprise. Toward the end of the performance, a suggestion of conventional four-beat meter creeps in, but it never becomes definitive. In sum, "Murder Most Foul" is a soaring artifact that eludes capture. In its very uniqueness, this extraordinary late-career milestone is as representative of Bob Dylan's achievement as any other work celebrated in this book.

5

BOB DYLAN AS COMPOSER, II

Musical Form

In the arts, giving form to a work is an essential task of any creator, if the work is to have accessible shape and coherence, and therefore meaning. A composer employs the elements of music—rhythm and pitch, primarily—to create significant forms, and it follows that musical form has actually been under discussion throughout much of this book so far, and especially in the preceding chapter. Still, nothing seems to strike fear more readily into the hearts of unschooled music lovers than to initiate a consideration of musical form.

Let me assure an uneasy reader that anyone perceiving the arc of a melody or an alteration of rhythm, or responding to the difference between a chord of tension and a chord of arrival, is hearing musical form. Form, as such, generally implies a consideration of such elements on the scale of an entire piece, rather than in terms of local details. But this consideration need not pose difficulties, especially in the case of songs, where we have the lyrics to assist with a discussion of the essential aspects of form: overall organization, and the roles of repetition and contrast in creating formal patterns.

Strophic Form: The Virtues and Challenges of Repetition

Strophic form is the most basic of formal patterns for a song. With strophic form, a unit of music is used repeatedly for successive stanzas of lyrics.

The perfect, and perhaps the ultimate, example of a strophic song is "One Hundred Bottles of Beer on the Wall."

It might initially seem that a strophic song is the easiest kind to compose, but this is true only insofar as quality is a negligible matter. Strophic songs over- or underburdened with words, or with music utterly lacking in character, *are* easy to write. But a good strophic song requires a melody line that is memorable in itself, rather than merely generic, while also being flexible enough to accommodate effectively different sets of lyrics. It also requires a lyricist who can tailor multiple stanzas to suit the same music, respecting appropriate syllabification and prosody (accentuation). Anyone who thinks doing so a simple task is invited to attempt writing the next "Girl from the North Country" or "Blowin' in the Wind."

Strophic form is, of course, extremely common in folk music, and it is not surprising that Dylan adopted it as a compositional strategy for his earlier efforts. He not only adopted it, he *adapted* it—both by basing original songs on preexisting models, as is well known, and by playing creatively with the internal dynamics of the form itself, as will be shown. What is significant is how much artistic mileage Dylan was able to extract from this very basic formal approach. He continued to employ strophic form throughout his songwriting career, producing songs that ranged from three stanzas ("Blowin' in the Wind," from *The Freewheelin' Bob Dylan*, 1963) to forty-five stanzas ("Tempest," from the album of the same name, 2012), and he did not record a single song that departed from strophic form until "Ballad of a Thin Man," from his sixth album (*Highway 61 Revisited*, 1965).

"Don't Think Twice, It's All Right" (from *The Freewheelin' Bob Dylan*) amply demonstrates Dylan's skill as a strophic song composer. It merits a very thorough examination from this standpoint.

The opening section of "Don't Think Twice, It's All Right" reveals a very convincing synergy between the lyrics and the music, establishing a model that remains in place for the duration of the song. The lyrical stanza consists of eight lines, and the musical setting Dylan provides is eight phrases long, with the phrases clearly separated by rests in the vocal part. There are four stanzas in all, and the words for stanzas two, three, and four parallel the lyrical structure of the first to an extent that assures the maintenance of a convincing text-to-music relationship.

In the music, the first and third phrases are the same, reflecting a pattern in the lyrics established by the first stanza, where the first and third lyrical lines are identical ("It ain't no use to sit and wonder why, babe"). Having established this text-music symmetry, Dylan maintains it for two further stanzas, so that the listener will expect the pattern to prevail to the end. He then achieves a fine effect by shattering expectation in the final stanza: here, instead of the anticipated lyric repetition of "So long, honey babe," the third line/phrase is the searing "Goodbye is too good a word, babe." Strophic songs can seem very predictable, which paradoxically allows an astute artist to exploit anticipated predictability.

Continuing with the music for "Don't Think Twice, It's All Right," it will be noticed that the second and fourth phrases lie considerably lower in the singer's range than the first and third. This provides an effective setting for the second and fourth lines of lyrics in each stanza, which offer bitter, sometimes ironic asides to the sentiments expressed in the first and third lines—as when "It ain't no use to sit and wonder why, babe" is followed by "If you don't know by now" in the first stanza; or when "It ain't no use in callin' out my name, gal" is offset with "I can't hear you anymore" in the third and fourth lines of the third stanza. The fifth and sixth musical phrases are melodically parallel but are accompanied by different chords, reflecting the accumulating meaning and tension in the corresponding lyrics of each stanza (in stanza one, "When your rooster crows at the break of dawn,/Look out your window and I'll be gone"; in stanza four, "I ain't sayin' you treated me unkind,/You could have done better but I don't mind"). The penultimate line of lyrics in each of the stanzas provides the first of two punch lines ("You're the reason I'm trav'lin' on," stanza one; "We never did too much talkin' anyway," stanza two; finally and brutally in stanza four, "You just kinda wasted my precious time"), and the musical setting for these appropriately reverses the direction of the two previous ascending phrases, lingering on a repeated note and then dropping down. The final lyrics in each stanza state the same, ultimate punch line: "Don't think twice, it's all right," and the melody falls to its lowest note, as deflated as the singer himself. (In his recorded performance of the song on the *Freewheelin'* album, Dylan speak-sings these lyrics upon each occurrence, in what sounds like the vocal equivalent of a sneer.)

In the foregoing description of this song, I have alternated prioritizing musical and lyrical structure, and this was deliberate. Songwriters are often asked which comes first, the words or the music. But in the best songs, words and music seem to exist in an inseparable fusion, to an extent that the question appears to be completely beside the point. This is surely the case with "Don't Think Twice, It's All Right." And it is worth stressing that such fusion does not result from fortuitous happenstance; it is the mark of highly attentive, exceptional songwriting. We may find analogous artistry in many of Bob Dylan's songs, where the synergy between music and lyrics may be understood and admired in a similar manner.

In "Blowin' in the Wind," for example, each of the three lyrical stanzas has an identical structure: three questions, followed by "the answer is blowin' in the wind." This justifies, even invites, a strophic musical form. The melodic phrases for the three questions are closely similar, with the last few notes of the second altered to provide some variety, but none of them comes to rest on the home (tonic) note of the scale; that resolution is provided only for the final, "answering" phrase of the lyrics. "Blowin' in the Wind" and "Don't Think Twice, It's All Right" share the lyrical device of having each stanza end with the same words, a refrain that, in effect, provides a mini-chorus for the songs.

Bob Dylan's strophic songs include many that lack mini-choruses, with new words throughout for each lyrical stanza. A few of the better-known ones are "Girl from the North Country" (from *The Freewheelin' Bob Dylan*), "Just Like Tom Thumb's Blues" (from *Highway 61 Revisited*), "I Dreamed I Saw St. Augustine" (from *John Wesley Harding*, 1967), and "If You See Her, Say Hello" (from *Blood on the Tracks*, 1975). Nevertheless, having the conclusions of lyrical stanzas in strophic songs rhyme with, or echo, one another is a favorite strategy of Dylan's. Once established as a pattern within a song, it builds anticipation and provides release lyrically, complementing the musical resolution that comes with the ends of strophes. Almost every Dylan album will provide several examples of this practice: from *The Times They Are a-Changin'* (1964), the title song, "One Too Many Mornings," and "Only a Pawn in Their Game"; from *Blood on the Tracks*, "Tangled Up in Blue," "Simple Twist of Fate," and "Shelter from the Storm"; and the list could go on.

At times, Dylan could even invert this procedure. In the strophic song "Political World" (from *Oh Mercy*, 1989), it is the *first* line of lyrics, containing the title words, that remains identical from strophe to strophe. And in "Duquesne Whistle" (from *Tempest*), both the opening and penultimate lines of each long strophe present the song's title ("Listen to that Duquesne whistle blowin'"—occasionally varied to "Can't you hear that Duquesne whistle blowin'?"), with the same melodic line, creating in effect a kind of recurring lyrical and musical frame for every strophe.

When several lines of lyrics get repeated from stanza to stanza within a song, a separate subsection, or formal *chorus*, is created. Within the stanzas, the subsections with changing lyrics are then referred to as *verses*. Songs with a verse-chorus structure may be regarded as extensions of the strophic principle, where the strophe has expanded to a two-part form.

Verse-Chorus Structures

The chorus becomes an especially prominent feature in a song when it receives a musical setting that makes it clearly distinct from the verses. A fine example of this is the well-known chorus of "Like a Rolling Stone." Clearly set off by preceding long notes in the vocal line—"scrounging for your next *meeeaaal*," "do you want to make a *deeeaaal*," and so forth—the chorus arrives with the virtual hue and cry of "How does it feel?" and the long-delayed harmonic resolution to a tonic chord. Big, anthemic choruses like this are relatively rare for Dylan, although one may find other instances (from the 1976 album *Desire*, "Joey" comes to mind). "Day of the Locusts" (from *New Morning*, 1970) offers a special case, where the chorus ("And the locusts sang") seems to recall (or invite?) an insect singalong. In this four-strophe song, the chorus lyrics in the second and fourth strophes differ somewhat from those in the first and third. But Bob Dylan is not a man to go by a strict rulebook, despite what would appear to be his considerable fondness for repetition.

Songs with verse-chorus forms have an obvious advantage over simpler strophic forms, insofar as they provide greater musical variety. But the separable, repeating chorus requires a sufficient justification of its own. Form becomes a dry, academic matter unless it is linked to a work's meaning and expressivity.

"A Hard Rain's a-Gonna Fall," from the *Freewheelin'* album, is the first appearance on record of a Bob Dylan song with a verse-chorus structure. The chorus becomes an identifiable subsection because of the many repetitions of the words "(and) it's a hard" before the title lyrics are heard in full to conclude the strophe. The lyrical importance and effectiveness of this is obvious, but there are musical reasons why the chorus stands out as well. The arrival of the chorus presents the first new development in the melody line after several repetitions of the same musical phrase, repetitions that set the several answers to questions posed by the opening lyrics of each strophe. For example, the first strophe begins by asking "Oh, where have you been, my blue-eyed son?/Oh, where have you been, my darling young one?" Five answers follow, starting with "I've stumbled on the side of twelve misty mountains," each of them sung to the same music. When "and it's a hard" finally arrives, the music takes a fresh melodic and rhythmic turn, clearly setting off the chorus and reinforcing the significance of its lyrics. The effective melodic and harmonic design of the chorus in "A Hard Rain's a-Gonna Fall" was previously discussed in chapter 4.

"Hard Rain" rewards serious attention not only because it demonstrates the way in which a chorus may be crucial to the lyrical and musical essence of a song. It also reveals two major compositional strategies that Dylan continued to employ fruitfully.

First is the construction of effective and accessible structures for extensive strophes, through the creation of identifiable subsections within the long units. In effect, "Hard Rain" consists of *three*-sectioned strophes, two-sectioned verses followed by choruses, with the lyrical and musical subdivisions reinforcing one another. Each of the song's five strophes has the two opening questions (and notice the parallel musical lines for the two, with the second one ending on an unresolved note and chord, as if awaiting the answers); then the group of answers, distinguished by a new musical line that is repeated for each answer; and finally we hear the words and music of the chorus. Multisectioned strophes, musically and lyrically partitioned by means analogous to those just identified in "Hard Rain," occur frequently in Dylan's output. Among many fairly straightforward examples of this are "Like a Rolling Stone," "Idiot Wind" (from *Blood on the Tracks*), "Black Diamond Bay" (from *Desire*; see chapter 4), and "Jokerman" (from *Infidels*, 1983).

Even among these four, however, are interesting differences. "Like a Rolling Stone" and "Jokerman" have traditional choruses. "Black Diamond Bay" has no proper chorus, but the conclusion of each long strophe with the title lyrics makes, one might say, a gesture toward the notion of a chorus. With "Idiot Wind," the last subsection of each strophe seems to *sound* like a chorus, introduced as it is with a break in the vocal line followed by the title lyric, arriving with a tonic chord. Significant lyric changes occur within this subsection from strophe to strophe, however, and in the final strophe even those lyrics that had previously remained unaltered (beginning with "Idiot wind, blowing every time you move your teeth") are replaced with new ones ("Idiot wind, blowing through the dust upon our shelves"). The alteration of the concluding lines, marking the point at which the singer, despite his raging anger, comes around to faulting himself along with the woman in their broken relationship ("We're idiots, babe"), achieves a devastating impact.

The second strategy revealed in "Hard Rain" is one that I will call the *variable strophe*, or the expandable strophe. It is heard when a repeated melodic phrase within a strophe is used a different number of times from strophe to strophe, to accommodate a different number of lyrical phrases. In the case of "Hard Rain," the number of answers to each pair of questions changes. At first there are five answers, with the corresponding musical phrase heard five times. Then, in the second and third strophes, the number of answers increases to seven. In the fourth strophe, it decreases to six. The unpredictability creates a rising tension within what would seem to be a static form; this is true both within strophes and as the song progresses from strophe to strophe, as the listener awaits the chorus each time and then wonders how many answers will lie within the next section. It is masterful of Dylan to use the factor of musical repetition—which logically would seem to increase the listener's capacity for boredom—to paradoxically engender a developing sense of involvement and, in the case of this frightening song, even anxiety.

In the fifth, final strophe of "Hard Rain," there are no fewer than *twelve* answering phrases, yielding both lyrical and musical culmination as the singer responds to the ultimate question, "What'll you do now?" The wait for the chorus seems interminable yet overwhelming, as the references to empty hands, "pellets of poison," the prison, the executioner, hunger, all pile up, yet what real release can the falling hard rain possibly bring? Bob Dylan has here taken a strategy of song structure readily associated with additive comedy (consider the twelve drummers drumming, eleven pipers piping, ten lords a-leaping, etc., etc., etc. of "The Twelve Days of Christmas") and put it convincingly in the service of a tragic vision.

When Dylan employs the strategy of the variable strophe in a verse-chorus song, it is typically the verses of the song that get altered in length. Instances of this may be found in "The Lonesome Death of Hattie Carroll" (from *The Times They Are a-Changin'*) and "Mr. Tambourine Man" (from *Bringing It All Back Home*, 1965). In "Like a Rolling Stone," however, Dylan adds a new phrase to the *chorus* beginning in the second strophe, inserting into it the now-famous line "with no direction home" (see chapter 1).

"Mr. Tambourine Man" is another celebrated Bob Dylan song that, like "A Hard Rain's a-Gonna Fall," displays verse-chorus structure within three-sectioned strophes of variable length. Like so many of Dylan's finest works, this one offers exceptions to the traditional rules. Here the chorus is heard first. And the music for the chorus is identical to that used for the lyrics of the verses. As it happens, these two factors are intricately interrelated.

In terms of the lyrics alone, the opening words of the chorus, "Hey! Mister Tambourine Man," provide a memorable verbal hook, enticing the listener into the song in a way that could not be matched by the opening of the first verse ("Though I know that evenin's empire has returned into sand"), its poetic intensity notwithstanding. But the musical rationale for leading with the chorus is even more compelling. This rationale is best understood by reviewing the musical developments as sequentially experienced by the listener.

The opening chorus itself consists of four brief phrases, the first and third of which are lyrically and musically identical ("Hey, Mister Tambourine Man, play a song for me"). The second phrase ("I'm not sleepy") ends unresolved, melodically and harmonically, while the final phrase ("In that jingle jangle morning") resolves to the tonic note and chord; the pairs of phrases present a kind of call-and-response relationship. It is the first two phrases of the chorus that supply all the musical material for the verses to follow. (The remarkable effectiveness of Dylan's chord choices in this song receives thorough attention in chapter 4.)

The first verse of "Mr. Tambourine Man," immediately following the opening chorus, itself consists of two identical subsections, each of which musically reiterates the first two phrases of the chorus—with a single addition. The addition—on the words "vanished from my hand" in the first subsection, and on "(I) have no one to meet" in the second subsection—comes from the melody notes setting "play a song for me" in the chorus. Here we see what is achieved by having the chorus come first: the music for the first verse can now be heard as an *expansion* of the chorus music heard initially. And this in turn sets forth a *process* that continues in the ensuing verses, as more expansions using those same melody notes lengthen and enrich the song (in the second verse, "[My] senses have been stripped," "[My] hands can't feel to grip," "[My] toes too numb to step," and so on). The process culminates in the fourth and final verse, where each subsection offers *four* such expansions. The effect of drawing out, even suspending, the sense of passing time complements beautifully the wish for escape, for fading, for disappearing, that is so memorably articulated by the lyrics. The many musical repetitions engender a hypnotic effect over the course of the entire song, while the whirling imagery fixates the listener's attention.

Had Dylan set up "Mr. Tambourine Man" in a traditional verse-chorus format, with the first verse preceding the chorus, the chorus music would be heard as a compression of the verse music. This conventional choice might possibly have been effective in its own way, but it would have foreclosed the experiencing of the verses as expansions of the chorus. Even more important, such a choice would have obligated the listener to wait for the end of the second strophe in order to identify the chorus as a *chorus*, the repeated lyrics being necessary for the identification in this case, where the various musical parts of the strophe are so similar. "Mr. Tambourine Man" reveals Bob Dylan as a song composer who can masterfully manipulate seemingly minimal materials of melody, harmony, and form to create works of startling originality and impact.

Building Bridges

The songs on Bob Dylan's first five albums are all strophic in form, some with choruses, and some without. On his sixth album, *Highway 61 Revisited*, "Ballad of a Thin Man" is the only song to break this mold. Starting out as if it will be a strophic song, as expected, "Ballad of a Thin Man" surprises with a brief bridge section—defined as such by the new music that accompanies the new words, beginning with "You have many contacts"—following the third strophe. After the bridge, four additional strophes, musically identical to the first three, are heard, and the song fades out.

Why did Dylan feel the need to add a bridge to "Ballad of a Thin Man"? The long strophes already have the internal variety created by the presence of a chorus ("Because something is happening"), and Dylan obviously hadn't felt that his previous long songs required such a contrasting section. Perhaps the fresh music here, with the vocal melody positioned in a consistently high register, helps illuminate the lyrics' change of perspective at this point. The scene shifts to the world outside the room/show/circus(?) where "Mister Jones" is undergoing his experience/inquisition/education(?), and we learn of the lumberjacks who provide him with "facts." This "outside" perspective is retained for the following strophe, with its references to professors, lawyers, and books, before we are abruptly shifted back "inside," in the company of a sword-swallower and a mysterious midget, for the duration of the song.

Bridge sections naturally provide additional musical variety to any song, and there is also the sense of musical roundedness resulting from the return to the main music of the song after the bridge. When the musical novelty of a bridge section is paired with some new development in the lyrics, the formal structure of the whole becomes particularly satisfying. Dylan obviously seemed to be investigating this possibility with "Ballad of a Thin Man." His subsequent album, *Blonde on Blonde* (1966), reveals a marked new interest in experimenting with the incorporation of bridge sections into his songs. It's as if Dylan were asking himself which songs might have bridges, how many sections overall should songs with bridges have, and even, how many bridge sections might be placed into one song.

The traditional A-A-B-A formal structure (where "B" is a bridge section) is found among the *Blonde on Blonde* songs in "Just Like a Woman" and in "Most Likely You Go Your Way and I'll Go Mine." In "Just Like a Woman," an unexpected harmony lends intensity to the start of the bridge, and that intensity is soon furthered by the lyrics, with references to "dying there of thirst," "your long-time curse," and "this pain in here." The ending of this bridge section literally creates a "bridge" over to the succeeding section, musically and lyrically, by means of the phrase "Ain't it clear that—[new section] I just can't fit." (This is an unusual practice for Dylan, whose bridge sections typically form discrete units.) With "Most Likely You Go Your Way and I'll Go Mine," it is the lyrics that shift abruptly to announce the bridge, introducing a judge who holds a grudge. Both of these songs have A sections that include choruses; in each case, the chorus prominently features the title words of the song.

"I Want You" is similarly structured, to the extent of including choruses in the A sections, except here Dylan adds another section to end the song, producing an A-A-B-A-A form. The bridge is set off lyrically by the turn to "all my fathers" and "all their daughters." "Temporary Like Achilles" shares this five-part structure, but in this case the bridge is set off harmonically as well as lyrically, with a shift to minor chords and the singer's self-characterization as a "poor fool."

Probably the most unconventional of the *Blonde on Blonde* songs from a formal standpoint is "Absolutely Sweet Marie," in which the bridge music occurs *twice*, with different words each time, as part of an overall A-A-B-A-B-A-A structure. The music of the bridge certainly bears repeating, with its sudden, striking beginning on a totally out-of-key chord. For all the appropriate attention and admiration that Dylan's song lyrics from this stage of his career have garnered, it seems evident that an adventurous, broadening approach on his part to musical form was a simultaneous development during this period.

With a wide range of formal possibilities now available to him, Dylan's evolution from this point remained, typically, unpredictable. The next album of new material after *Blonde on Blonde* was *John Wesley Harding* (1967), dominated by brief, gnomic songs lacking bridge sections, but that was followed in 1969 by *Nashville Skyline*, in which every new composition featured a prominent bridge section—including the instrumental "Nashville Skyline Rag." From *New Morning* (1970) onward, it would be characteristic of Dylan to employ a variety of song forms on a single album.

"Something There Is About You," from *Planet Waves* (1974), finds Dylan introducing, for the first time in his work, a striking hybrid form that in effect synthesizes strophic principles with A-A-B-A structures. Here, each strophe consists of four long lines of lyric, set to music in which the third line breaks the melodic and harmonic pattern of the other three, functioning like a mini-bridge section *within* the substantial strophe. The song's four strophes themselves then become miniature song forms within the overall structure. (This hybrid form occurs elsewhere in popular song; one well-known example is the Beatles' "Eight Days a Week.") An additional subtlety of this overall structure in "Something There Is About You" is Dylan's melodic variation of the third strophe: the harmonic and rhythmic patterns remain the same as in the other strophes, but the voice employs a higher register, musically reflecting the intense emotion as "the spirit in me sings" and the singer asserts to his loved one "You're the soul of many things." Arguably this variation creates another, large-scale A-A-B-A structure among the four strophes.

The strophic song with A-A-B-A strophes recurs in Dylan's more recent work. Two examples from *Modern Times* (2006) are "Spirit on the Water" and "Beyond the Horizon." In both these songs, the B music within the strophes accompanies once again a change in the lyrics' direction—in the first stanza of the former, "I'd forgotten about you"; in the first stanza of the latter, "I'm touched with desire." Another example of this formal strategy, from *Tempest*, is "Pay in Blood," which also utilizes the concluding line of each strophe as a mini-chorus: "I pay in blood, but not my own."

Bob Dylan's interest in using formal bridge sections to add variety to his song structures is still evident in his most recent work. The 2020 album *Rough and Rowdy Ways* offers two examples. The opening song, "I Contain Multitudes," begins as if it will be a strophic song, but then it broadens out into an elaborate A-A-A-B-A-A-B-A structure. Variety is achieved in the B sections with a striking move toward minor in the harmony, with the beat becoming much more prominent in the accompaniment. As would be expected, the bridge sections also mark new directions in the lyrics; the first one brings sudden references to Anne Frank, Indiana Jones, and the Rolling Stones, and the second veers abruptly to address "You greedy old wolf."

The fourth selection on *Rough and Rowdy Ways*, "I've Made Up My Mind to Give Myself to You," begins as if it will be a typical A-A-B-A love song but proceeds to present an even more elongated structure than "I Contain Multitudes": the pattern would be represented as A-A-B-A-A-B-A-[instrumental] B-B-A. The instrumental bridge section is particularly unusual for Dylan. Once again, the bridge sections shift to minor and to a fresh rhythmic articulation, and they provide further structural variety insofar as they are half the length of the A sections (while giving the aural impression that the tempo has doubled, with the lyrics being delivered twice as fast). In this case, however, the lyrics for the bridge do not significantly depart from the prevailing tone or spirit of this gentle song of devotion. The song is among the tenderest in Dylan's entire output and one that offers an alternative to the frequently dark and sometimes philosophical character that typifies other songs on *Rough and Rowdy Ways*.

Some Notes on the Blues

The blues has been an essential reference point so far throughout this book. The centrality of the blues to Bob Dylan as a performer received attention in chapters 2 and 3. Blues is no less central to Dylan as a song composer, but in regard to form it is important to recognize that there is no one standard blues form. Rather, blues is best understood as a complex of lyrical, musical, and performative practices that may be employed, or referenced, in part or as a whole, as flexibly as the creative imagination allows. Blues elements may be present in strophic songs, in songs with verse-chorus structures, and in songs with bridge sections. Focusing briefly here on Dylan's use of blues elements in his compositions will open a fuller appreciation—of the enormous influence blues traditions have exerted upon him, and in turn, of the extent to which he has contributed to the continuing importance of those very traditions.

In its lyric structure, the archetypical blues stanza has three lines, with the second literally repeating or echoing the first and the third providing an answering or punch line. (See the discussion of "What Was It You Wanted?" in chapter 3.) The three-line stanzas typically follow one another, to produce shorter or longer strophic forms when set to music. Dylan has written songs in this format throughout his career, from the early 1960s ("Down the Highway," from *The Freewheelin' Bob Dylan*) to the 2000s ("Rollin' and Tumblin'," and "The Levee's Gonna Break," both from *Modern Times*; "Shake Shake Mama" from the 2009 album *Together through Life*). Included in this group are such varied works as "Ballad of Hollis Brown," a harrowing account of poverty and violence (from *The Times They Are a-Changin'*); the idiosyncratic love song "She Belongs to Me" (from *Bringing It All Back Home*); the country-flavored "Down Along the Cove" (from *John Wesley Harding*); the blatantly erotic "New Pony" (from *Street Legal*, 1978); the gospel-preaching "Gonna Change My Way of Thinking" (from *Slow Train Coming*, 1979); the deceptively simple, ultimately cryptic "10,000 Men" (from *Under the Red Sky*, 1990); the lonely but determined "Dirt Road Blues" (from *Time Out of Mind*, 1997); and the mood-shifting "Lonesome Day Blues" (from *"Love and Theft,"* 2001).

Dylan's music for his traditionally formed blues lyrics is as varied as the imagery and emotions conveyed by the lyrics themselves. "Ballad of Hollis Brown" has an unrelenting minor-key coloring; "She Belongs to Me" is brightened by its major key and gentle beat; "Gonna Change My Way of Thinking" hammers its message home via a minor key and an aggressive rock beat; "Dirt Road Blues" has an echo-tinged, rockabilly-like flavor; and so forth. Many of the songs with this familiar lyric structure directly borrow traditional chord progressions and rhythmic patterns associated with the blues, but others reveal a more fluid relationship to those musical conventions. "Ballad of Hollis Brown" has no harmonic movement at all, displaying a kinship to some of the rawest rural blues, while "She Belongs to Me" has a chord vocabulary slightly different from that of a standard three-chord blues.

That standard three-chord vocabulary is linked to what musicians call "twelve-bar blues," a specific rhythmic and harmonic framework for the three-line blues stanzas. In twelve-bar blues, every line of lyric receives four rhythmic units (bars, or measures) of four beats each, composing a total of twelve such units for each stanza, and there is a specific chord progression typically associated with this rhythmic organization. Simply put, every stanza begins on the tonic chord, and the second and third lyric lines within the stanza then arrive with a chord change, followed by a return to the tonic within these lines. Different chords are used to begin the second and third lines, and so in its most straightforward form the twelve-bar blues employs a three-chord vocabulary. The standard chord progression in twelve-bar blues positions the chord built on the fourth degree of the scale (the subdominant) at the start of the second lyric line (bar five) and positions the chord built on the fifth degree of the scale (the dominant) at the start of the third lyric line (bar nine).

This is of course just a basic template, honored by musicians frequently in the breach as well as in the observance. Nevertheless, scores of songs demonstrate this classic twelve-bar blues organization. The compatibility of the harmonic plan with the traditional three-line blues stanza is evident: it assures that the lyric repetition in the second line will be freshened by different music, and that the crucial third line will have its own distinctive harmony. (It is also a framework that can serve independently of lyrics for instrumental blues pieces.)

Bob Dylan employs the twelve-bar blues framework both with his traditionally formed blues lyrics and in songs with other lyric patterns. Among the songs listed previously as examples of the standard pattern, "Lonesome Day Blues" offers as prominent a presentation of basic twelve-bar blues as could be desired. The one-two-three-four beat, with a heavy backbeat on two and four, is foregrounded throughout the recording, and the chord changes on bars five and nine of every stanza, along with the returns to the tonic on bars seven and eleven, may readily be heard. Another blues tradition, that of call-and-response between voice and instrumental accompaniment, is evident in every four-bar phrase of the song, as Dylan's gravelly vocal (yet another blues tradition) alternates consistently with a recurring, forceful instrumental riff. "The Levee's Gonna Break" presents another obvious illustration of twelve-bar blues, this one without the elaborate call-and-response of "Lonesome Day Blues." In "The Levee's Gonna Break," Dylan creates larger patterns from the repetitive blues stanzas—lyrically, by having the line "If it keep on rainin' the levee gonna break" return at intervals, and musically, by placing an instrumental twelve-bar blues stanza after every fourth vocal stanza.

An example of Dylan pairing a musical twelve-bar blues with a different pattern of lyrics is offered by his big 1966 hit, the whimsically titled "Rainy Day Women #12 & 35" (released as an abridged single, then as the lead-off track on the *Blonde on Blonde* album). The bass drum pounds out every beat, making the rhythm and the chord changes easy to follow. Although the lyrics are not in an archetypical blues format, they can be seen as reflecting the influence of that format, as the opening lines of each stanza repeat "They'll stone ya when," leading to the punchline "I would not feel so all alone, everybody must get stoned" (which is reiterated at the end of each stanza, functioning like a mini-chorus within the blues structure).

Within Dylan's output, the music of twelve-bar blues gets paired with all kinds of lyrics. The diversity is reflected in such notable examples as the smiling-in-the-face-of-adversity "Buckets of Rain" (from *Blood on the Tracks*), the apocalyptic "Man of Peace" (from *Infidels*), and the desolate, yearning "Million Miles" (from *Time Out of Mind*). The latter two, like "Rainy Day Women #12 & 35," end each of their stanzas with identical lyrics; Dylan is obviously fond of this mini-chorus effect, which occurs also in the late twelve-bar blues song "Crossing the Rubicon" (from *Rough and Rowdy Ways*). In the case of "Million Miles," the darkly colored lyrics find a musical counterpart in a minor-key version of the twelve-bar blues progression, a pairing that also characterizes the song "Beyond Here Lies Nothin'" (from *Together through Life*). Finally, the twenty-stanza "Highlands," which concludes *Time Out of Mind*, demonstrates all by itself the virtually limitless ways in which Bob Dylan can utilize the twelve-bar blues formula: to tell any kind of story, to evoke all manner of imagery, and to enhance any mood. (*The Definitive Bob Dylan Songbook* presents "Highlands" as a twenty-four-bar structure, representing each measure of twelve-bar blues as two measures, probably in order to make Dylan's brief, rapidly articulated vocal phrases easier to read in music notation.)

A whole book could easily be devoted to the influence of the blues on Bob Dylan (and vice versa). That influence is so pervasive throughout Dylan's career, as performer as well as composer, that it is difficult to delineate its boundaries. "Subterranean Homesick Blues" (from *Bringing It All Back*

Home) follows the three-chord harmonic progression of classic twelve-bar blues but spreads the progression out over an irregular eighteen-bar span. The lyrics do not correspond to any traditional blues pattern. It might seem a stretch therefore to connect this song to the blues, yet Dylan invites us to do so by featuring "blues" in the song title, and of course his vocal performance is replete with blues-derived chanting and inflections. The title song from *Highway 61 Revisited* does not even have "blues" in its title, but it raises the same kinds of issues because of its chord progressions, vocal line, and recorded performance (in this case, both vocal and instrumental performance; the guitar and electric keyboard parts prominently feature blues licks).

Considerations of the less obvious influences the blues may have exerted on Bob Dylan may rapidly devolve into arcane hair-splitting. Is it significant that the epic "Desolation Row," the magnum opus that concludes *Highway 61 Revisited*, employs harmonic progressions having clear ties to twelve-bar blues, in spite of its not being in any real sense a blues song? Although in Dylan's most recent album, *Rough and Rowdy Ways*, the chord progressions and rhythms of twelve-bar blues persist as an obvious framework for just two of its ten songs ("Goodbye Jimmy Reed" and "I Crossed the Rubicon"), how important is it to note that identifiable, if less distinct, echoes of the harmonic and phrase structure of twelve-bar blues may be traced in at least three of the other songs? Does it really make sense even to pose such questions? Rather than engage such matters, it seems safest to posit that such questions *will* arise, as the understandable and inevitable consequence of the fact that the blues is such an essential component of Dylan's vocabulary—as musician, as lyricist, and as performer. Other components are present and frequently assert themselves. But nothing supersedes the blues in enduring importance for Bob Dylan.

6

ACCOMPANYING BOB DYLAN

Instruments, Instrumentalists, Singers

The distinctive sound world of particular Bob Dylan songs has inevitably played a role in preceding discussions: the intense and path-breaking double keyboard (piano and organ) textures introduced in "Like a Rolling Stone" and the barren landscape evoked by the dark bass and drum accompaniment to "As I Went Out One Morning," to cite just two examples. In its sheer, simple *sound*, Dylan's output offers a cornucopia of variety and expressivity. Sometimes the sound of an entire album will be defined by Dylan's singular choice of accompanying musicians—violinist Scarlet Rivera on *Desire* (1976), for instance, or the members of The Band on *Planet Waves* (1974). These two albums, and many others could be added, do not sound at all like each other, or like any other Dylan studio albums. For that matter, they do not sound much like any other albums by anybody.

Dylan's sensitive and highly individual ear for sound will be celebrated briefly in this chapter. The technical aspects of performance and production need not concern a listener and will not concern us here. Rather, I will attempt to probe the ways in which Dylan's decisions about his own accompanying instruments (acoustic guitar, electric guitar, piano), and his other accompanying musicians, help to shape and enrich the listener's experience of his work.

As a solo performer on his first four albums, Bob Dylan's instrument of choice for accompanying his singing voice and his harmonica was the acoustic guitar, with a single exception. Dylan accompanies himself with piano in "Black Crow Blues" on *Another Side of Bob Dylan* (1964). Otherwise, Dylan showcases himself as a highly competent guitar player, who often employs his instrument not simply to provide harmony and rhythm but to enhance the emotional coloring of his songs.

From the listener's standpoint, the two basic acoustic guitar sounds are those of picking (individual notes) and strumming (chords). The best-known songs on Dylan's second album, *The Freewheelin' Bob Dylan* (1963), demonstrate his use of the possibilities of these accompaniments. Most often, he mixes picking and strumming, as in "Blowin' in the Wind." But in "Masters of War," Dylan employs consistent, unrelieved strumming, which maximizes the somber intensity of this protest against the inhumanity of which humanity is capable. Contrariwise, gentle fingerpicking dominates the accompaniment of "Girl from the North Country," contributing to the song's air of poignancy. Fingerpicking can also sound more aggressive, however, as it does on "Don't Think Twice, It's All Right," where the consistent rhythmic impetus of Dylan's guitar provides a musical counterpart for the restless desire to move on that is expressed in the song's lyrics.

Another particularly effective use of the acoustic guitar is heard in "Ballad of Hollis Brown" from *The Times They Are a-Changin'* (1964). Here, a repeating four-note pattern on the low strings of the guitar emerges immediately in the instrumental introduction and recurs in the guitar response to every vocal phrase. The cold, metallic sonority of this figure, combined with the static harmony, engenders an oppressive feeling of droning doom, reflecting in music the hopelessness of Hollis Brown's story.

With a full arsenal of guitar techniques at his disposal, why might Dylan have turned to the piano for "Black Crow Blues"? He certainly had plenty of previous experience providing guitar accompaniments for blues-oriented songs. I do not have an evident answer for this. Yet Dylan's accompaniment for "Black Crow Blues" is certainly pianistic, evoking the boogie-woogie piano style with its active left-hand rhythms; there is no obvious guitar analogy. There is no guitar equivalent either, of course, of Dylan's sweeping glissandos on the piano. And the very clipped, staccato piano sound surely accords with the "kickin', tickin'" nerves Dylan sings about. Dylan's recorded keyboard debut might be less noteworthy were it not for the very prominent role the piano was to assume in his later work—played both by himself and by others.

First, though, came the seemingly momentous change to an electric band accompaniment on side one of the *Bringing It All Back Home* LP (1965). Despite the consternation and even outrage occasioned by the choice, it has more than one obvious rationale. (See the discussion of Dylan's "rocker" voice in chapter 2.) Change itself may have been one motivation; on the album's "Outlaw Blues" Dylan even justifies his wish to be "on some Australian mountain range" solely on the basis of its being "some kind of change." The acoustic bluesman slips seamlessly into an electric environment in the twelve-bar blues songs "Outlaw Blues," "On the Road Again," and "Bob Dylan's 115th Dream." And "Subterranean Homesick Blues" and "Maggie's Farm," which are protest songs as surely as any of Dylan's acoustic numbers in that category, protest that much more vehemently in the rock setting. In his own liner notes for *Bringing It All Back Home*, Dylan states that "my songs're written with the kettledrum in mind/ a touch of any anxious color." Although Dylan generally eschews *kettle*drums, drums do occupy a regular and important position in his sound world from 1965 onward, and his electric ensembles certainly contribute more than "a touch" of "anxious" coloration.

The effectiveness with which Dylan could utilize his accompanists may be heard throughout his second album released in 1965, *Highway 61 Revisited*. A strong drum stroke kicks off the record with "Like a Rolling Stone," and drums continue to be prominent: from the pounding back beats at a breakneck tempo in "Tombstone Blues," to the admirably appropriate chugging rhythms in "It Takes a Lot to Laugh, It Takes a Train to Cry," and on through the album. Keyboards now assume a central role, as piano and organ both are immediately foregrounded in "Like a Rolling Stone" and remain essential elements in the sound architecture of *Highway 61 Revisited*, creating different musical environments for different songs. For example, "Ballad of a Thin Man" opens with the piano playing a distinctive minor-key chordal pattern, establishing a darkly colored atmosphere, and the organ joins in shortly thereafter in a much higher register, where it remains throughout—hovering spookily over the proceedings, with occasional long trills and abrupt accents. In this song, the organ evokes a bizarre synthesis of a circus calliope with the sound of an old-time horror movie score, both very suitable for lyrics depicting a hapless and clueless "Mister Jones" encountering a geek, a sword swallower, and a one-eyed midget. And in the following song, "Queen Jane Approximately," the two keyboards execute a complete change of musical scene. The tinkly, high-register piano passages, consisting of ornamental melodic figures that would not be out of place in a cocktail lounge (such as might be frequented by the very proper "Queen Jane"), complement the organ's high chordal covering, which would not be out of place in a contemporary daytime television soap opera (such as the Queen might have faithfully watched).

Of course, the role of the electric guitar in *Highway 61 Revisited* should not be minimized. Michael Bloomfield's slashing guitar fills following the stanzas of "Tombstone Blues" and "Highway 61 Revisited" are especially memorable and contribute in no small part to the intense, fraught ethos of these songs, bringing a gritty immediacy of feeling to Dylan's metaphoric, often surrealistic lyrics. In the title song, "Highway 61 Revisited," Dylan even allows himself a rare special effect: what the album credits call a "police car" (actually a slide whistle) that is heard at points along this "highway." Finally, after all the varied and pioneering additions to his sound world presented in the first eight tracks of the album, Dylan achieves an equally distinctive effect by cutting back abruptly for the big, long final selection, "Desolation Row." No keyboards, no drums, no big electric rock sound here. Just Dylan, his harmonica and acoustic guitar, minimal accompaniment, and eleven-plus minutes of dazzling lyrics and musicality. This back-to-basics approach to a concluding album track is heard also on *Slow Train Coming* (1979); "When He Returns" features only Dylan's vocal and Barry Beckett's piano.

In his subsequent albums, Dylan would sometimes set a particular song apart from its surrounding tracks by selecting the piano rather than the guitar to accompany himself. The pleading, personal tone of "Dear Landlord" would distinguish it in any case from the other songs on *John Wesley Harding* (1967), but certainly Dylan's piano contributes musically to its individual qualities. The remarkably wide harmonic (and vocal) range of "Dear Landlord" also sets the song apart from any others on the album and might render it more suitable for the piano than for the guitar; it is intriguing to ponder whether its chordal vocabulary was the result of the song's piano orientation, or vice versa. Another example of a number highlighted in the context of its album by Dylan's piano is "Dirge," from *Planet Waves* (1974). The accusatory, disparaging tone of "Dirge," encompassing both the singer and his ex-lover ("I hate myself for lovin' you"), is unique on *Planet Waves* and virtually demanded an unexpected musical setting.

The only other instrument heard on "Dirge" is the guitar, whose striking melodic lines, set in counterpoint to Dylan's vocal, are played by Robbie

Robertson of The Band. Members of The Band already had a long history with Bob Dylan by the time of *Planet Waves*, having played with him during his extensive world touring in late 1965 and the first half of 1966, and having also worked with him during his long period of retirement from the road and recuperation from a motorcycle accident in 1967, when the informal tape recordings now known as the "basement tapes" were made. Selections from these recordings—never intended for commercial release at the time—eventually appeared on the double LP *The Basement Tapes* (1975) and on Dylan's *Bootleg Series*, volume 11 ("The Basement Tapes, Raw," 2014). The mutual experiences and obvious compatibility of Dylan and The Band are reflected in the singular atmosphere and virtuosity evident on *Planet Waves*, starting right from the outset with the rambunctious, manic, yet tight groove established on "On a Night Like This." Garth Hudson's accordion part adds immeasurably to the flavor of this opening number, as does his organ playing elsewhere on the album—especially on "Tough Mama," where Levon Helm's drumming contributes equally to the power of this singular song of seduction. The memorable melodic character of Robbie Robertson's guitar playing is evident on "Going, Going, Gone," "Something There Is About You," and the slow version of "Forever Young," as well as on "Dirge." Dylan once again sets his final song, "Wedding Song," apart by means of instrumentation; here, he performs solo, with just his harmonica and his acoustic guitar, emphasizing the utterly personal nature of the piece.

Having the piano-centered number be the exception on an album is Bob Dylan's typical procedure, but this is intriguingly reversed in the case of *New Morning* (1970), on which the sound of the piano—played mostly, but not exclusively, by Dylan—dominates the album, and the guitar-centered songs prove to be the exceptions. That Dylan actively experimented with his choice of instruments in preparing *New Morning* is documented by several tracks on the fascinating 2013 release *Another Self Portrait* (*The Bootleg Series*, volume 10). Evidently Dylan started out with "Time Passes Slowly" and "Went to See the Gypsy" as guitar-accompanied songs, deciding only later in his compositional process that he wanted to play piano on them both. The reverse process seems to have taken place with "If Not for You," which became the opening track for *New Morning*. *Another Self Portrait* offers a version of "If Not for You" with Dylan on vocals and piano—and an accompanying violinist. This appealing anomaly assumes a weirdly prophetic character in light of the essential role the violin would come to play years later on *Desire*.

New Morning also prominently features a chorus of three female backing singers on several selections. They add obviously appropriate sweetening to the mock-sentimental "Winterlude" and, even more appropriately, three angelic voices to the conclusion of Dylan's spoken-word "Three Angels." The chorus also lends a gospel-like suggestion to the album's final song, "Father of Night." (The function of the female chorus on "Sign on the Window" and "The Man in Me" is something that I find elusive.) One of the singers contributes a scat-singing accompaniment to Dylan's other spoken number, the jazzy "If Dogs Run Free."

Any listener surprised by the sonic novelties on *New Morning* could be directed to the album that preceded it by just a few months, *Self Portrait* (1970). It is true that *Self Portrait* is an album consisting mainly of cover versions and arrangements of folk standards; nevertheless, the variety of instrumentation employed throughout the album is both striking and indicative, as is the use of female backing singers. The utterly enigmatic opening track, "All the Tired Horses," is a Bob Dylan original performed not by Bob Dylan, but by female chorus and a large group of instrumentalists, dominated by a string section with other orchestral instruments. The continuously shifting accompaniment, swelling gradually and then receding, is the source of (considerable) interest here, as the lyrics simply repeat unceasingly.

Dylan would continue to use female backing singers to a considerable extent on many of his albums from the 1970s and 1980s. The first of them to employ backing singers on every selection is *Street Legal* (1978)—forecasting, in effect, the gospel-chorus sounds that would permeate Dylan's Christian-themed albums *Slow Train Coming* (1979), *Saved* (1980), and (to a significant extent) *Shot of Love* (1981). These gospel-style albums feature the women in ways both obvious and inventive. Call and response is an essential aspect of gospel style, and Dylan and his backup singers certainly engage in this, from the first track on *Slow Train Coming*, "Gotta Serve Somebody." A particularly imaginative approach to this procedure may be heard in "Pressing On," from *Saved*. This is another instance in which repetition of lyrics invites—or perhaps we should say demands—an arresting musical counterpart.

In "Pressing On," the frequently repeated chorus section (referring here to form rather than to performers—this is a song with verses and a chorus) begins the song and consists of not much more than repetition itself, of the words in the title. The section is heard three times in a row. First, Dylan performs it solo. The second time through, the backing singers offer initially a tentative response and then join Dylan for the final words ("To the higher calling of my Lord"). Next, the women become more active and more interactive with Dylan—a two-faceted process that continues throughout the rest of the song. After the first verse, the women add "on and on and on and on" to previously open spaces in the chorus section between the restatements of "pressing on." Eventually, as the final chorus sections occur and fade out, the backing singers are contributing continuous, ecstatic vocal ornamentation, producing the richest musical textures of the song. Pressing on, indeed! In this instance, neither a lyric sheet nor the basic sheet music would reveal the principal source of interest. The accompanying singers are, along with Dylan, really the indispensable focal points of "Pressing On," as the background becomes the foreground.

The album *Desire* (1976) features many vocal duets, pairing Bob Dylan on most of these with Emmylou Harris, and on "Hurricane" with Ronee Blakley. Vocal duets with female artists recur in Dylan's albums of the 1980s. But what is most remarkable about *Desire* is not the accompanying singers, it is the accompanying *violinist*, a unique occurrence on Dylan's studio albums. Dylan performs two selections on the album as vocal solos ("Isis" and "Sara"), but the violinist, Scarlet Rivera, is present on every track. And not just present—Rivera is prominent throughout, to an extent that would justify calling *Desire* an album of duets for voice (or voices) and violin. Additional justification for this comes from the fact that, unlike Dylan's vocal partners, who perform in synchronized harmony with him as would be expected, Rivera creates an improvised counterpoint of independent violin lines, enriching all the songs on *Desire* with added strands of melody. This aspect of the album is sufficiently unusual to warrant a bit of close examination.

It must be emphasized that Rivera is no country fiddler; she is a classically trained violinist, which accounts for the distinctive flavor of her contributions to *Desire*. The opening track, "Hurricane," suggests immediately the important role that she will play. Her violin is the first voice heard, entering before the start of Dylan's vocal and just after the key and tempo have been established. She plays a brief, memorable melodic figure that rotates around four adjacent notes of the scale—a kind of cross between a classical motif and a pop-song hook—that comes to function as a repeated reference point throughout the song. There are only brief interruptions in the violin's prominence, as Rivera accompanies the vocals and leads the instrumental breaks between stanzas. Initially, as Dylan's singing begins, the violin's presence is obvious yet understated, but Rivera participates in an increasingly active and arresting fashion. After the first vocal stanza, the violin part in the break jumps abruptly higher in pitch. The second instrumental break finds Rivera playing elaborate ornamental figures in a high register, as if reacting anxiously to the lyrics' depiction of the cops arriving in the "hot New Jersey night." A total of ten instrumental breaks occur between stanzas in "Hurricane," and each of the ten violin parts is different from the others, either subtly or significantly.

The following track, "Isis," also demonstrates effective organizational strategies. The violin is first heard in the breaks between stanzas. When Dylan's harmonica joins in the break after the third stanza, a striking harmonica-violin duet results, after which Rivera comes to accompany Dylan's vocals as well. Harmonica-violin duets recur at points throughout "Isis" and are a feature of other songs on *Desire*, perhaps most notably "Oh, Sister."

There is no song in which the violin contributes more to forging an uncanny, and in this case chilling, musical atmosphere than "One More Cup of Coffee (Valley Below)." Here, the violin entrance once again precedes the vocal, setting a somber tone in the instrument's low register (before ascending to the higher register that will characterize much of its music in this song) and moving at an elegiac slow tempo. There is an open, sparse sound that does not abate with Dylan's vocal entrance; Rivera's high-register violin parallels and complements Dylan's own distinctly high-register singing, and their accompanying instruments remain subdued throughout most of the song. When Emmylou Harris joins Dylan for the brief chorus sections in this verse-chorus song, it only adds to this exotic reinvention of a high lonesome sound. The instrumental conclusion finds the violin playing eerie, rapid melodic decorations, as if embodying the "mysterious and dark" lady to whom the song is addressed, whose pleasure "knows no limits," but whose voice is "like a meadowlark."

This chapter offers only an initial suggestion of the wealth to be found within the musical textures of Bob Dylan's albums. Like so many avenues of exploration introduced in this book, the topic merits much further investigation, and it is hoped that the preceding discussion provides a few productive models for such investigation. Dylan's accompaniments are an underexplored subcategory within the larger underexplored subject of Bob Dylan as a performing musician.

7

ARRANGING AN ALBUM

In preceding chapters, the characteristic sound-print of certain Bob Dylan albums—the accompaniment by The Band on *Planet Waves* (1974); Scarlet Rivera's violin and the vocal duets on *Desire* (1976)—and the positioning of individual songs on his albums—"Desolation Row" as the clear "finale" to *Highway 61 Revisited* (1965); the two versions of "Forever Young" on *Planet Waves*—have received attention. Ample evidence suggests that Dylan gave some thought both to the sequencing of songs on his recordings and to the overall impact of that sequence. Were we still in the time when the LP was the predominant medium for listening to recorded music, the topic of arranging an album would obviously be of major significance. Now, however, with even CDs rendered obsolete for many listeners in an age of downloads, music streaming, and YouTube, this potentially rich subject might seem a distant anachronism, of interest only from a historical standpoint, if that. Nevertheless, it merits our attention, because listening to Bob Dylan's songs as *albums*, in their intended sequence, and even allowing for the two sides of the original LPs, can enhance the listener's experience of his work.

From the beginning of his career, Bob Dylan, like other folk performers of his generation, was primarily an album artist. Dylan has had hit singles, but they are sidelights; his commercial distinction is as one of the best-selling album artists of all time. Indeed, as his career progressed, the increasing duration of many of his songs virtually demanded the LP format. By the time of *Blonde on Blonde* (1966), Dylan had seemingly outgrown even the single-LP format, with "Sad-Eyed Lady of the Lowlands" occupying an entire side of this double-record production. Yet the traditional album arrangement surprisingly reasserted itself with *John Wesley Harding* in late 1967: a single LP, with six songs to a side, many of them with a timing of less than three minutes. Dylan's songs began to grow longer again beginning with *Planet Waves*, but for two decades thereafter he remained comfortable with the typical single-LP format for all his studio albums.

The first Dylan album that seems to have been conceived more as a CD than as an LP is *Time Out of Mind* (1997). With a playing time just short of seventy-three minutes, *Time Out of Mind* could not have fit on an LP. (The album was in fact released on vinyl, but as a two-record set.) Even without the epic concluding track, "Highlands" (duration 16+ minutes), the album ran longer than any released by Dylan since *Desire* in 1976. And on *Time Out of Mind*, Dylan, working with producer Daniel Lanois, made uncharacteristic use of a modern digital studio, employing sampling of rhythmic patterns, along with distortion and other studio effects. Conceived in an age when listeners to the CD could specify their own selective programming of tracks, or choose a random shuffling of them, *Time Out of Mind* nevertheless, and ironically, reflects as profound a level of thought about album unity and sequencing as any Dylan recording from the decades when the LP format defined the field. It serves perfectly to illuminate the advantages of listening to a Bob Dylan album as a complete, purposeful program of individual songs.

Time Out of Mind opens with the sonic equivalent of a picture coming gradually into focus: a softly emerging, vague chordal environment; isolated guitar notes; the suggestion of a pulse, picked up by regular, repeating minor chords played on the organ; and finally the entrance of Dylan's voice. The singer articulates in words the physical and emotional landscape that has just been evoked by the sparse, slowly plodding music: "I'm walking . . . through streets that are dead." "Love Sick" serves as a highly effective opening track, but it also sets a tone, musically and lyrically, for the entire album to follow.

With a single exception, the songs on *Time Out of Mind* are darkly colored. Three of them are in minor keys ("Million Miles," "Can't Wait," and "Love

Sick"), but Dylan's vocal blue notes give minor shadings even to many of those nominally in major keys. The obvious blues coloring of "Love Sick" foreshadows the centrality of the blues to the album. The very particular sound world of "Love Sick" establishes another point of departure for the album as a whole: its rather spectral, open, but pulsating sonority recurs very specifically in "Million Miles," but obvious and subtle permutations of its texture and timbre are readily to be heard in many of the other songs as well. As is frequently the case with Dylan albums, a particular group of musicians plays on every track, helping to ensure a continuity of approach throughout the album, and Dylan's consistently craggy voice works in peculiar but convincing harmony with them. Another source of unity comes from the systematic occurrence of long pauses in the vocal lines of several songs, pauses that stand out in the spare sonic environment that dominates *Time Out of Mind* and that serve to underline the poignant emotional environment of the songs. These pauses permeate the vocal part of "Love Sick" and may be heard to equally telling effect on "Standing in the Doorway," "'Til I Fell in Love with You," "Not Dark Yet," "Cold Irons Bound," "Can't Wait," and "Highlands."

Lyrically, *Time Out of Mind* is dominated by somber, even despairing songs, and the motif of a journey through darkness that is established by "Love Sick" persists in other numbers. "Love Sick" begins specifically with the singer walking, and the following two songs, "Dirt Road Blues" and "Standing in the Doorway," both commence in the same fashion (with "Gon' walk down that dirt road" and "I'm walking through the summer nights," respectively). Journeying continues with the next track, "Million Miles" ("I'm tryin' to get closer but I'm still a million miles from you"), and the motif may be traced, in specific or symbolic terms, right up to the concluding "Highlands," where the singer's ultimate destination stands revealed: "Over the hills and far away/There's a way to get there and I'll figure it out somehow." It could be argued that even the anomalous track "Make You Feel My Love" implies a journey yet to be completed, the goal being the beloved's acceptance of the pleading singer, who would go "crawling down the avenue" and beyond, "to the ends of the earth."

In arranging the order of the tracks on any album, considerations of variety along with unifying factors are important if a satisfying listening experience is to be provided. That *Time Out of Mind* works well in this regard may be illustrated simply by the opening two tracks. "Dirt Road

Blues" continues the blues orientation and the dark journeying theme of "Love Sick," but the invigorating—even danceable—tempo, the infectious blues riff played by the guitar, and the thicker instrumental texture all create ample contrast with the opening number. The combination of dour lyrics with spirited music in "Dirt Road Blues" may seem paradoxical, but it's a classic blues paradox. One particularly effective juxtaposition in the sequencing of *Time Out of Mind* is heard as the eighth track, "Cold Irons Bound," gradually comes to life after the immediately preceding "Not Dark Yet" has succumbed to encompassing gloom. The juxtaposition aligns perfectly with the corresponding lyrics. At the end of "Not Dark Yet," the singer can't even hear "the murmur of a prayer," whereas the opening words of "Cold Irons Bound" are "I'm beginning to hear voices." As for the positioning of the mock-epic "Highlands" at the conclusion of the album, how could anything possibly follow that blues marathon? Its final lyrics, stating that the singer has reached the highlands in his mind, if not physically, "and that's good enough for now," offer as provisionally optimistic an ending as could be appropriate for an album like *Time Out of Mind*.

"Make You Feel My Love," a reasonably conventional song of romantic yearning, might appear out of place on *Time Out of Mind*. Its lyric content aside, Dylan sets it apart musically. It's the only track on which he plays piano and the only song on the album with a traditional pop-song A-A-B-A form. Positioned well past the halfway point if one is listening sequentially, it certainly fulfills the function of contrast by separating two dark and blues-drenched songs ("Cold Irons Bound" and "Can't Wait"). It is worth noting here that there are other instances on Dylan albums where a fairly consistent overall tone, lyrically and musically, is broken—I would assume deliberately—by a song that presents a striking contrast, somewhere beyond the halfway point. On *The Times They Are a-Changin'* (1964), the triumphant "When the Ship Comes In," stands apart in an album of sober political and social commentary and songs about broken (or breaking) relationships. And the intimate personal ambience of *Blood on the Tracks* (1975) is interrupted by the long western fantasy "Lily, Rosemary, and the Jack of Hearts."

The preceding observations about *Time Out of Mind* offer avenues of investigation into other Bob Dylan albums from the standpoint of integrated, patterned listening experiences. Both *The Times They Are a-Changin'* and *Blood on the Tracks* feature well-chosen opening and closing tracks and characteristic sound-prints, in addition to the focus on a particular tone and subject matter that was just mentioned.

The Times They Are a-Changin' begins with its title song, defining the political and cultural climate that will be further explored in numbers like "With God on Our Side," "North Country Blues," "Only a Pawn in Their Game," and "The Lonesome Death of Hattie Carroll." Interspersed among these are equally intense songs of personal disappointment: "One Too Many Mornings" and "Boots of Spanish Leather." "Restless Farewell" provides the obvious conclusion to *The Times They Are a-Changin'*. Dylan signs off by assuring us that he will make his stand, remain as he is, "And bid farewell and not give a damn"—not exactly a warm and fuzzy valedictory, but one totally in line with the unsentimental, penetrating tone of the entire album. (Taking sequential listening to another level, it is fascinating how well "Restless Farewell" prepared the Dylan album that was to follow later in 1964, *Another Side of Bob Dylan*, in which Dylan moved forcefully away from the specific contemporary focus of *The Times They Are a-Changin'*, alienating many fans at the time who might have wished to freeze him in the limited role of topical songwriter and protest singer.)

Since *The Times They Are a-Changin'* is an acoustic solo album, a basic musical unity is automatically present. Dylan provides variety, however, with the changes in tempo, in the guitar patterns, in the degree of rhythmic flexibility from one number to the next, and with his choice to employ the harmonica or not in a particular selection.

In the case of *Blood on the Tracks*, "Tangled Up in Blue" opens the album effectively, plunging the listener into a complex world of interpersonal relationships that are characterized by intense feelings, missteps, and unfulfilled longing—a description that could be applied equally well to many of the songs that follow. Although it was recorded with different musicians at different times and in different places, *Blood on the Tracks* is, for the most part, a relatively subdued-sounding album musically, as suits the intimate subject matter. "Tangled Up in Blue" establishes the model for this as well; despite the presence of a band, the accompaniment is gentle, with acoustic guitars at the forefront. Several songs on *Blood on the Tracks* feature an acoustic Dylan with only bass accompaniment (Tony Brown). The recurrence of this distinctive duo provides an ongoing source of musical unity, and this is the instrumentation employed for the album's two final tracks, "Shelter from the Storm" and "Buckets of Rain." "Buckets of Rain" concludes the album in the spirit of sweet-tempered resignation. While granting that life is "sad" and "a bust" (no surprise, after the overriding tone of the preceding songs), the singer nevertheless ends by assuring his loved one that he'll do whatever he must do for her, "honey baby, can't you tell?"

The two big exceptions to a delicate sound on *Blood on the Tracks*—one on each side of the original LP, as it happens—are "Idiot Wind" and "Lily, Rosemary, and the Jack of Hearts." These points of strong contrast also stand apart lyrically, the former for its angry and rather vindictive message, and the latter for its foray into third-person storytelling. The LP of *Blood on the Tracks* also provides an effective ending for side one, with the reluctant farewell song "You're Gonna Make Me Lonesome When You Go," and an equally apposite recommencement for side two, with the anticipated reunion of "Meet Me in the Morning."

The experience of the double-sided LP record may well appear an arcane consideration at this point in the history of music recording and distribution. Nevertheless, the enforced pause between songs over a side-break on an LP was an unavoidable part of the listening experience back in the day, and it was something that canny artists designing an album could consciously use to their advantage. The side-break separating the two versions of "Forever Young" on *Planet Waves* was discussed previously in chapter 4. *Bringing It All Back Home* (1965) was clearly a two-sided conception, with electric rock songs on side one and basically acoustic sounds on side two. The songs on side one are all relatively short (under four minutes), except for the hallucinatory "Bob Dylan's 115th Dream," which provides a larger-scaled conclusion to the side, and virtually demands a measured pause to prepare the vastly different musical experience—and four long songs—on side two. Side two achieves its own, definitive conclusion with the aptly titled "It's All Over Now, Baby Blue."

For the reader who wishes to pursue the vinyl experience, still available as of this writing (although not the default mode of listening to be sure), two more particularly satisfying examples of side-breaks will be offered. Listening to *Highway 61 Revisited* on LP, we leave Mister Jones in "Ballad of a Thin Man" fading out on side one, only to find his equally clueless female counterpart, "Queen Jane Approximately," greeting us on side two. And on the *John Wesley Harding* record, the "Drifter's Escape" provides a fine conclusion to the first side, while offering a refreshing pause before Dylan surprises us on piano with "Dear Landlord" at the beginning of side two.

The CD releases of Dylan LPs certainly have their conveniences, and some listeners may prefer the sound quality, but it is always relevant to keep in mind the sound medium for which an artist originally intended his work.

Bob Dylan's CDs of the 2000s have, like so many of his earlier albums, featured consistently fine backing musicians. In particular, the presence of the multi-instrumentalist Donnie Herron and of bassist Tony Garnier on every release from the 2006 *Modern Times* up to the 2020 *Rough and Rowdy Ways* has assured a consistency of musical approach both within and among the albums. This group of albums would include the holiday album *Christmas in the Heart* (2009) and the three albums of classic pop songs *Shadows in the Night* (2015), *Fallen Angels* (2016), and the three-disc *Triplicate* (2017), along with the albums of original material (*Together through Life*, 2009; *Tempest*, 2012; and *Rough and Rowdy Ways*). The obvious affinity shared by Dylan with Herron, Garnier, and other musicians with whom he has toured as well as recorded extensively, is evident and contributes substantially to the pleasure of listening to these CDs as integrated wholes. This returns us to the matter of characteristic sound-prints that distinguish and unify Dylan albums, for which additional earlier examples could well be cited. I am thinking here especially of distinctive rhythm sections: the team of Charlie McCoy (bass) and Kenneth Buttrey (drums), equally at home in the spare environment of *John Wesley Harding* and the ample country landscapes of *Nashville Skyline* (1969); and that of reggae masters Robbie Shakespeare (bass) and Sly Dunbar (drums), who lend a memorable punch to every track on *Infidels* (1983).

Bob Dylan's most recent album, as of this writing, is the two-CD *Rough and Rowdy Ways*. This release serves as notice that Dylan's attention to the overall ambience of an album, and to the sequencing of its individual songs, has if anything become more prominent, even as he approaches his eightieth year. Perhaps the least expected, yet obvious, feature of *Rough and Rowdy Ways* (given the title of the album) is the persistence of a gentle, meditative musical tone, established at the outset by "I Contain Multitudes" and sustained throughout much of the album, with only the occasional departures created by more aggressive-sounding numbers ("False Prophet," "Goodbye Jimmy Reed"). "I Contain Multitudes" sets the mold: an intimate, relatively smooth vocal delivery; a rhythmic fluidity in the singing that is encouraged here by the absence of drums and, in many of the sections, only the subtlest feeling of a regular beat; and an uninterruptedly soft dynamic level in both the vocal and its instrumental accompaniment. On disc one, these exact characteristics also inform "Black Rider," and "Mother of Muses" and "Key West (Philosopher Pirate)" are cut from similar musical cloth. "My Own Version of You" and "I've Made Up My Mind to Give Myself to You" also retain the understated aesthetic, while providing variety in rhythmic treatment and instrumental color. "Crossing the Rubicon" occupies a kind of halfway house between the quieter and the more emphatic selections: each of its many stanzas begins with strong, percussive instrumental attacks and relatively loud singing but then relaxes decisively for the remainder of the stanza.

From a musical standpoint, *Rough and Rowdy Ways* might appear an ironic title for an album of this character. Yet there are rough edges aplenty in the song lyrics, which arguably stand out the more against the musical restraint that typifies so many of the numbers. Not a minute's time has passed for the listener before the singer in "I Contain Multitudes" claims, in his first rhyme for the song title, "I fight blood feuds."

The radically unconventional "grand finale" to *Rough and Rowdy Ways* is "Murder Most Foul," which occupies the entirety of disc two. (Prior to its release on the album, "Murder Most Foul" was unleashed by Dylan on an unsuspecting internet in early spring 2020.) This song shares the basic mold of "I Contain Multitudes," with the exception (like "Mother of Muses") of employing percussion for color, rather than for marking a steady beat. "Murder Most Foul" could have fit on disc one without exceeding the time limitation for single CDs. Why, then, did Dylan separate it out onto a clearly labeled "disc two"? Perhaps to offer listeners the unexpected, and for some nostalgic, experience akin to turning over an LP record or of reaching for the second record in a two-LP set? In any case, it does seem that "Murder Most Foul," as fine a conclusion as it is for *Rough and Rowdy Ways*, requires some aural space both before and after it, space that is certainly provided by its sole placement on a CD of its own. Its length and its unusual musical and lyrical qualities, discussed previously in chapter 4, set it apart, even from anything else in Dylan's remarkably diverse output. A unique ending for a unique album, "Murder Most Foul" attests to a creative mind still functioning at full tilt, in the organizational strategies for presenting work to the public as well as in the strategies for fashioning the work itself.

8

BOB DYLAN IN LIVE PERFORMANCE

Documenting a Musical Shape-Shifter

I can change, I swear
—Bob Dylan, "You're a Big Girl Now,"
from *Blood on the Tracks* (1975), and on
Hard Rain (live performance, released 1976),
and in numerous other live performances
(probably more than two hundred additional
times, 1976–2007) officially unreleased

In "You're a Big Girl Now" the words "I can change, I swear" are a lover's plea—when removed from that context, they could well serve as Bob Dylan's artistic credo. Dylan thrives on live performances of his work, and those live performances in turn thrive on the freshness brought by his willingness to experiment with that work. Dylan's career over the last several decades has been largely defined by what has come to be called his "never-ending tour," and a study of his songs in concert performances would require a book of its own—doubtless a book considerably longer than the present one. The frequency with which Dylan changes his songs when performing them live arguably sustains his life as a creative artist, while assuring his fans' continuing engagement and more than occasional consternation.

Dylan began officially releasing live performance albums in 1974 with *Before the Flood*, a two-record set documenting his tour with The Band. Since then, numerous official releases have made significant selections from Dylan's concert work widely available, especially with the advent of *The Bootleg Series* beginning in the 1990s. Although the focus of this book is the studio albums, it makes no sense to ignore the other material completely, and some listeners may take considerable interest and pleasure in comparing official studio and live concert versions of individual songs. To provide examples of such comparisons, this chapter will briefly examine five distinctive songs, beginning with the one that provides the epigraph for this chapter, "You're a Big Girl Now."

A relatively short time separates the release of "You're a Big Girl Now" in studio performance from its sole official release in concert performance (as of this writing), yet the differences between these two versions are extensive. As a composition, the song is a painfully intimate creation, obviously addressed to one very specific "you": the singer (a very specific "I") is "singin' just for you" and even identifies just where he can find "you"—in somebody else's room. The studio performance on *Blood on the Tracks* preserves the intimate feeling, with a gentle, muted arrangement that emphasizes acoustic guitar, soft piano, and discreet drums. Dylan's singing here tends toward the quietly expressive, but the affecting cries of "oh, oh" in the middle of each stanza resound as if the deep hurt he is trying to keep under articulate control must ultimately find some outlet in preverbal form. The artifice of the record album allows a listener to indulge the illusion that she is in a private situation, with Dylan singing just to "her," whoever she conceives that person to be. The delicate harmonica solo at the end sustains the mood, and the song fades out, remaining finally as unresolved as the singer's emotional state.

To bring such an intimate song to the live concert stage is inevitably to alter its basic character. The illusion of individual-to-individual communication cannot be sustained. But the very public performance of supposedly personal love songs is a staple of our musical culture, and were Dylan to omit such songs from his concert repertoire he'd have to leave behind a substantial and impressive portion of his output. The concert performance of "You're a Big Girl Now" on *Hard Rain* creates, in several respects, a song different from that heard on *Blood on the Tracks*. The subtleties of the studio would not translate effectively to the concert venue, with its heavy rock instrumentation and an actively engaged audience that is clearly in evidence on the recording. (In this context, it is worth noting that the studio "You're a Big Girl Now" even lacks a bass part.)

In concert, "You're a Big Girl Now" becomes a broad public testament to the singer's anguish, a kind of abstract plea hurled to a distant "big girl" who is not specifically present and may even be long gone. The tempo of the *Hard Rain* version is significantly slower than that heard on *Blood on the Tracks*—it could arguably be called dragging, as opposed to the more natural, conversation-like tempo Dylan used in the studio. But the choice is effective in a different way, as an expression of enduring pain. The loud instrumental punctuation on middle lines in each stanza—"And I'm back in the rain," "And I'm just like that bird," "I can change, I swear," and so on— helps to spotlight and isolate the singer on these crucial words. The vocal moans that follow these lines are now on "aay" instead of "oh," allowing Dylan wider-mouthed howls that, along with his generally louder and more intense vocal, assure a strong impact in a concert setting. The deliberately sluggish tempo permits the singer to draw out words at several points: the "I" on "I hope that you can hear" and "I can make it through"; "It's a *price* I have to pay"; "and, rather spectacularly, the "corkscrew" to the singer's heart in the final stanza.

The *Hard Rain* performance of "You're a Big Girl Now" changes some of the harmonies employed on the studio version. The most noticeable alteration is the avoidance of a completing cadence, melodically and harmonically, at the ends of stanzas. This is significant; instead of coming to rest musically, the voice at these points hangs in midscale, and rather than providing a tonic chord, the accompaniment drops out completely, leaving a hole of silence while the singer rests. These pauses were obviously intended to produce a remarkable and poignant effect. Unfortunately, crowd noise is audible right through each musical silence, compromising the expressive intent (and inadvertently demonstrating that what might be controllable in a studio cannot be controlled in a concert setting). After the interruptions, the band resumes, tentatively at first, and then entering forcefully with the missing tonic chord, preparing the next stanza, or providing the "missing" ending at the song's conclusion, no fade-out being feasible in a concert performance.

Perhaps much of the live recording of "You're a Big Girl Now" sounds heavy-handed and overblown in a private listening setting, yet there is one novel aspect of the performance that introduces a different kind of intimacy. This is the presence of Scarlet Rivera's violin, which achieves something akin to a personal commentary in the face of the rather impersonal band sound, bringing forth a fragile solo instrumental voice to complement by contrast Dylan's rough-hewn, impassioned singing. This comes through particularly during the instrumental break section, where the simple expressivity of the violin line penetrates right through the very busy guitar solo.

Bob Dylan is often inclined to change around the lyrics of his songs in live performance. Although there are no significant alterations to the words of "You're a Big Girl Now" between the studio and live recordings, the *Hard Rain* version exchanges the positions of the third and fourth stanzas of this five-stanza song. In the case of these nonnarrative lyrics, the new arrangement does not affect the substance of the song. Perhaps the intent may simply have been to keep those in the audience who were familiar with the released album version of the song on their toes. Those interested in the lyric changes that may occur from one version to the next of any Dylan song to be found on more than one of his albums may consult Bob Dylan's *The Lyrics*, edited by Christopher Ricks, Lisa Nemrow, and Julie Nemrow (New York: Simon and Schuster, 2014), a truly mammoth undertaking and achievement that is worth its considerable weight in gold to any true Dylan afficionado.

The release of the Bob Dylan *Bootleg Series*, besides making many previously unreleased live performances available, has also made many Dylan demos of his songs, along with discarded studio takes, rehearsals, alternate versions, and much other intriguing material, readily accessible. The deluxe edition of *The Bootleg Series*, volume 14, *More Blood, More Tracks* (6 CDs), enables a listener to trace a prehistory of "You're a Big Girl Now," from a Dylan acoustic demo to various studio takes in New York, all of which preceded the recording of the song in Minneapolis (December 1974) that was finally selected for the released album *Blood on the Tracks*. (One of the New York studio takes had previously been released in 1985 on *Biograph*.) Similar investigations may now be pursued for many other Dylan songs; in effect, one could construct their prenatal development and then their concert afterlife in relation to the presumably iconic studio recordings. But that would form the substance of yet another book.

For now, I will continue with comparisons between the studio recordings and selected, officially released concert performances of four other well-known songs. No effort toward completeness is attempted in the listings and discussions of live performances that follow. With new Dylan material appearing constantly, such an attempt might quickly become outdated in any case. My approach is selective, choosing for consideration accessible live recordings that illuminate matters of potentially significant interest for listeners.

Thinking More Than Twice about "Don't Think Twice"

Studio version: *The Freewheelin' Bob Dylan* (1963)

Released concert version 1: *Live 1964: Concert at Philharmonic Hall* (released 2004, *The Bootleg Series*, volume 6)

Released concert version 2: *Before the Flood* (Bob Dylan and The Band, recorded and released 1974)

Released concert version 3: *Bob Dylan at Budokan* (recorded and released 1978)

"Don't Think Twice, It's All Right" is one of Bob Dylan's songs that is both highly celebrated and widely performed (by Dylan himself, and by many others). I have examined this song previously as an example of Dylan's imaginative use of his harmonica (chapter 3) and as an instance of his masterful employment of strophic song form (chapter 5). It might initially be difficult to conceive of how Dylan's original studio version could be effectively changed. But Dylan's official website documents over one thousand performances of this song by its creator as of 2019, and the sampling of these offered by the three concert versions under review here suggests the extent to which he felt free to alter—even radically—his approach to it over time. This illustrates once again that Dylan views his work as continually evolving, multidimensional artifacts. No individual Dylan performance of a song, no matter how compelling (or not), should be seen as fixing that song in stone.

Of the three concert versions of "Don't Think Twice, It's All Right" being considered here, the first two are solo acoustic performances, and the third utilizes a band with electric instruments and backing singers. All three preserve the four stanzas of lyrics essentially as published in *The Definitive Bob Dylan Songbook*. (Curiously, they are not the exact words sung by Dylan in his studio performance on the *Freewheelin'* album: he alters some of the opening lyrics in the first stanza and substitutes "So long, honey babe" for

"I'm walkin' down that long, lonesome road, babe" as the first line in stanza four.) The differences among the three concert versions, and their individual departures from the studio performance, involve Dylan's singing style and his instrumental accompaniment.

The fundamental expressive character of "Don't Think Twice, It's All Right" is encapsulated in the irony of its title: the situation is emphatically *not* "all right," and the relationship the singer is leaving behind has failed because of his ex-partner's inability to behave thoughtfully. A distinguishing aspect of Dylan's studio performance of this song is that, while projecting assurance in his singing—there is little equivocation in the singer's decision to depart—the sense of bitterness is understated, and the irony of the reiterated title line is arguably the more effective for this approach. In contrast, the acoustic concert performances from 1964 and 1974 project their bitterness loud and clear.

In 1964, although he had yet to appear either on record or in live performance with a band, Dylan apparently was trying out his shouting stadium voice before the fact. The opening melodic line of each stanza in this "Don't Think Twice" is transformed so that it steadily ascends, calling out to the farthest reaches of Philharmonic Hall. This is akin to the later case of "You're a Big Girl Now," insofar as what was originally a person-to-person exchange (whether literally so, or just in the singer's mind) becomes here a public outcry and display. Dylan's singing is very self-conscious throughout this performance of "Don't Think Twice," teasing out key words for maximum impact ("look out your . . window . . and I'll be gone"; "I gave her my *heaaart*, but she wanted my *soouul*"), as if sticking pins precisely into a voodoo doll.

The role of the harmonica in this 1964 concert performance is equally transformed from that in the studio version. There is no longer the train-whistle color (see chapter 3), but the instrument is featured from the beginning, in an introduction preceding Dylan's vocal entrance, and is heard in a long solo between stanzas three and four; the harmonica also participates in a brief instrumental coda. The long solo is quite odd. It starts out following the underlying guitar harmonies of the vocal stanzas but appears to lose itself in brief repetitive phrases and wild swooping, eventually escaping even its harmonic and rhythmic bearings. The audience seemed to love it, however, as is evident from the cheering and applause heard on the recording, which raises questions. Was Dylan on this occasion using a song that was obviously already well known to his audience (much applause greeted the opening sung line) as a *vehicle*—for the exhibition of vocal and instrumental virtuosity? And was doing so planned from the outset, or was it a spontaneous outcome of the specific performing occasion? Regardless, by the end of the number Dylan was obviously enjoying himself; he nearly cracks up on the line "You just kinda wasted my precious time" as if amused by its expression of self-importance, and the guitar and harmonica seem just to collapse rather than give a proper, formal conclusion to the song.

A listener first encountering the 1974 concert recording of "Don't Think Twice" out of context, even a listener having some familiarity with Bob Dylan, might understandably wonder "Who's that singing?" On this selection, as well as on others on *Before the Flood*, Dylan must have consciously decided to deepen his vocal timbre. His singing sounds more robust and certainly less nasal than expected. The unwitting listener could be forgiven for wondering whether this might possibly be Elvis Presley imitating Bob Dylan—the truly prominent Dylan giveaways are the exaggerated vowels (especially on "don't think *twiiice*, it's all *riiight*"). Or perhaps it's an Elvis imitator imitating Bob Dylan, or even Bob Dylan himself imagining Presley imitating Dylan? In fact, Elvis Presley had recorded "Don't Think Twice, It's All Right" in 1971. Might Dylan have known Presley's performance? Although a very young Elvis Presley, when asked whom he sounded like, reportedly replied very appropriately, "I don't sound like nobody," Bob Dylan has demonstrated during his long career that he, in contrast, can sound like many different people.

In any case, Dylan's chosen vocal mask for his 1974 concert gave this "Don't Think Twice" a very dark intensity. The formal strategy is similar to that employed for the *Live 1964* performance: instrumental introduction (here with the merest hint of harmonica); a substantial harmonica solo between the third and fourth stanzas, serving to set off the final, definitive "fare thee well"; and an instrumental coda (here, a full stanza's worth of music, with the harmonica present throughout). Dylan enlarged on the melodic transformations in evidence on *Live 1964*, for many vocal phrases ascend into a forceful high register, lending an aggressive consistency to the interpretation. The harmonica solos also retain elements of the earlier concert performance, particularly the repeated figures and the high level of virtuosity, although things remained under more obvious control in 1974, and the song was given a definite, traditional conclusion. In sum, *Before the Flood* presents a distinctive, if rather impersonal "Don't Think Twice, It's All Right," suitable for a large stadium venue, and decidedly different from the familiar studio version designed basically for private listening.

Finally, the concert performance on *Bob Dylan at Budokan* certainly reveals another side of "Don't Think Twice, It's All Right." The elaborate band establishes a totally unexpected reggae rhythm at the outset, and the danceable, catchy quality, maintained from beginning to end, is underlined by the presence of a highly decorative flute part. There is no harmonica in evidence. Dylan sings the song straightforwardly, adhering by and large to the melody line he followed in his original studio performance. Within each of the stanzas, the first half is presented as a vocal solo and backing singers join Dylan for the second half. The arrival of the supporting vocalists is each time marked by rhythmic punctuations in the accompaniment, then the previous steady rhythm resumes for the last two lines of every stanza. The mini-chorus words, "don't think twice it's all right," are repeated at the ends of stanzas, emphasizing their chorus-like function.

In comparison with the other versions under discussion, the chordal vocabulary of this performance is changed and widened somewhat, contributing another source of musical interest. As in the two other concert recordings, there is an instrumental stanza preceding the final vocal one. The Budokan performance features an elaborate conclusion, with Dylan and the backing singers reiterating "it's all right" for emphasis, but any real sense of irony arguably is diluted by the upbeat feeling that endures.

From a purely musical standpoint, this is surely the most arresting, and possibly the most engaging, of the three live performances being considered. And it is apparent that the musical arrangement supports the basic structure of the song's lyrics. Still, the question arises, perhaps inevitably: what has this arrangement to do with the essential *character* of the song? Yet that question itself reveals the propensity to define the meaning of Dylan's songs solely in terms of their lyrics. By 1978, Dylan might have thought "Don't Think Twice" to be so overly familiar (to his listeners, as well as to himself) as to warrant treating it once again as a *vehicle*—but this time as a vehicle for musical imagination and experimentation. Whether an individual listener is willing to go along with him probably depends on the listener's own degree of familiarity with the song, and on how comfortable she might be letting go of the lyrics' profound expression of personal hurt in the interests of a musical surprise.

The remaining songs in this chapter will receive a more general treatment, highlighting the major points of expressive difference among various interpretations of the same selection.

"Just Like a Woman"—Which Woman?

Studio version: *Blonde on Blonde* (1966)
Released concert version 1: *Live 1966: The Royal Albert Hall Concert*
(released 1998, *The Bootleg Series*, volume 4)
Released concert version 2: *Live 1975: The Rolling Thunder Revue*
(released 2002, *The Bootleg Series*, volume 5)
Released concert version 3: *Bob Dylan at Budokan* (recorded and
released 1978)

"Just Like a Woman" offers an example of a song that Bob Dylan recorded with a band for its studio release but chose rather to perform as a solo acoustic number when he introduced it into his concert repertoire. The choice is significant, because Dylan was touring with The Band in 1966 and obviously had the option of using the group for the song—as he did with one other selection from *Blonde on Blonde* that is heard on the *Live 1966* album, "Leopard-Skin Pill-Box Hat." The choice of an intimate arrangement definitely affects the listener's experience of "Just Like a Woman."

This is not to say that the studio recording of "Just Like a Woman" lacks a feeling of delicacy—quite the opposite is true. Surrounded on the album by raucous arrangements (of "Leopard-Skin Pill-Box Hat" and "Most Likely You Go Your Way and I'll Go Mine"), the selection is notable for its understated accompaniment to Dylan's subtle and expressive vocals. Like "Don't Think Twice, It's All Right," "Just Like a Woman" is a song of regretful farewell. To what extent is this ambience preserved in live concert performances?

On *Live 1966*, Dylan seems intent, if anything, to exceed the sense of intimacy he had achieved in the studio. Instead of turning a very personal piece into a public statement (as he did with "Don't Think Twice" in 1964), Dylan sounds like he is retreating inward, singing as if he were unaware of any audience, and the audience for its part sounds subdued to the point of hanging on every word. For this particular audience (Manchester, England, May 17, 1966), *Blonde on Blonde* was as yet an unknown quantity, and the song doubtless was new to virtually everyone in attendance. Although the song ultimately is addressed to "you," Dylan creates the illusion of performing for the sole purpose of consoling himself; this performance represents that wonderful kind of paradox, a public presentation of very private feelings. The drawing out of vowel sounds, typical of Dylan generally and frequently exaggerated in his live performances, gives an impression in this instance of thinking out loud. (Notice, in the first verse, the "o" sounds especially: "kn*o*ws," "cl*o*thes," "b*o*ws"; and then in the bridge section "c*u*rse," "h*u*rts," and "w*o*rse.") At the ends of verses, when Dylan sings "[breaks just like a] little girl," the last two words fold into near silence, to heartbreaking effect. As in the studio version, the song concludes with an extensive harmonica solo, which here soars softly and repeatedly into the instrument's highest register: the musical image of the fragile girl-woman, and of the singer's attenuated, yet still piercing, feelings for her. (These observations also apply substantially to another live recording of "Just Like a Woman" from the same tour, now commercially available on *The Real Royal Albert Hall 1966 Concert*, released in 2016.)

The performance of "Just Like a Woman" on *Live 1975* turned in the completely opposite direction. This became a public celebration of what was by this time a well-known and well-loved song; in fact, we hear on the recording a member of the audience requesting the number just before the music begins, and the chorus words become literally singalongs for musicians onstage (and presumably for the audience as well). How this utterly extroverted approach, reflected in Dylan's own singing, affects the meaning of this confessional song of private pain is a matter I feel unprepared to address. In particular, the phenomenon of women participating in the choruses of a song with lyrics that some have found to imply misogyny could provoke some head-scratching. Perhaps it is best to suggest that, in this version, a Dylan song once again became a vehicle for a fresh kind of concert performance. The form of the song was reflected not only in the presentation of the choruses by a physical chorus, but in the forceful rhythmic accents, provided by the accompaniment, that set apart the bridge section. Dylan's intimate, poignant harmonica, which contributes so much to the flavor of the studio and *Live 1966* versions of "Just Like a Woman," clearly had no place in this rendition and is nowhere to be heard.

After the previously discussed arrangement of "Don't Think Twice, It's All Right" on *Bob Dylan at Budokan*, one might have expected to hear an equally idiosyncratic and outgoing approach to "Just Like a Woman" on that album. But with Bob Dylan you never can tell, and this 1978 performance of "Just Like a Woman" reverted to a delicate aesthetic, with a subdued accompaniment and a relatively soft, highly expressive Dylan vocal. Appropriately for this context, the harmonica returned, but Dylan effectively withheld it until his singing ended, after which it is heard providing a complete final verse and chorus—just as in the studio and *Live 1966* versions.

Dylan employed female backing singers for the Budokan performance, but his use of them was highly imaginative, from both lyrical and musical points of view. On the recording we hear the women enter on the choruses, but unobtrusively and very selectively—only for the exact words "just like a woman," leaving Dylan on his own to sing "just like a little girl." It's as if the backing group offers a shadowy remembrance for the singer of what this woman was like, but his notion of her breaking like a little girl belongs to him alone. The women also underline the bridge section with gentle background "aah" sounds.

Three Watchtowers

Studio version: *John Wesley Harding* (1967)
Released concert version 1: *Before the Flood* (Bob Dylan and The Band, recorded and released 1974)
Released concert version 2: *MTV Unplugged* (recorded 1994, released 1995)

"All Along the Watchtower" is a brief, compelling, and mysterious song. Its ominous character is captured memorably in the studio version, which utilizes for accompaniment just Dylan's guitar and harmonica, bass, and drums. The singing is utterly straightforward, as if recounting a simple parable about the nameless joker and thief; Dylan is not about to disclose a hint of any deeper meaning, and the effect is strangely telling. It falls to the instruments to depict the dark underside of the song: the active bass and drums in the interlude that precedes the final stanza foreshadow the galloping riders revealed in the lyrics to that stanza; and the wind-blown harmonica in the coda provides no real sense of resolution. The sustained minor key contributes strongly to the uneasy atmosphere.

Bob Dylan is known to have admired Jimi Hendrix's apocalyptically powerful interpretation of "All Along the Watchtower," and Dylan's own 1974 performance of the song with The Band surely reflects his admiration, capturing Hendrix's intensity without at all mimicking that celebrated cover version. Dylan and The Band establish a breakneck tempo, substantially faster than in either Hendrix's or Dylan's own studio recordings, and Dylan provides an aggressive, urgent vocal. Robbie Robertson's guitar solos each display an individual coloration, and the concluding one makes the wind not merely howl, but scream. The end comes with an abrupt, startling *major* chord that relieves at least some of the accumulated tension. On *Before the Flood*, "All Along the Watchtower" is transformed from a song of sinister suggestion into one of electrifying, overwhelming power.

For his 1994 *Unplugged* performance, Dylan returned to the moderate tempo of his original studio rendition. Vocally, he begins in an understated, almost conversational tone, with the accompanying band supporting him appropriately, allowing him the spotlight. The governing assumption might be that the audience knows this song well and that consequently Dylan can take a subtle approach to his singing, beginning in an almost non-committal fashion, so that all nuances will be noticed. On the recording, nuances soon begin to be heard, in the form of higher volume and drawn-out vowels on key words (such as "dig my *earth*," "it is *worth*," "but a *joke*," "not our *fate*," "getting *late*," and others). Particularly effective is Dylan's sudden marked change in vocal timbre for the last lines of the song, beginning with "Outside in the distance," underlining the shift in focus at this point. Dylan's final "howl" gradually accumulates intensity, leading to an extended instrumental coda—a section of its own, really—that surprises toward the end with an unprepared shift to a much slower tempo, and a gradually intensifying conclusion that could be heard to echo Dylan's last vocal gesture, culminating in the final minor chord. This is a thoughtful, touching "All Along the Watchtower" that shows Dylan refusing to take a seemingly modest twenty-six-year-old song of his for granted, or to use it simply as a showpiece. He is still pondering it, relishing it, and finding new avenues of expression through it.

"I Shall Be Released," Three Different Ways

Informal performance, with The Band (recorded 1967, first released in 1991 on *The Bootleg Series*, volumes 1–3, *Rare and Unreleased, 1961–1991*, later on *The Bootleg Series*, volume 11, *The Basement Tapes*, in 2014)
Studio version, with Happy Traum on *Bob Dylan's Greatest Hits Vol. II* (recorded and released 1971), later on *Biograph* (released 1985)
Released concert version on *Bob Dylan at Budokan* (recorded and released 1978)

The convoluted history of "I Shall Be Released" is due to the song's origins during the informal sessions Bob Dylan held with members of The Band in 1967, when he was in temporary retirement from studio recording and touring after a motorcycle accident the previous year. Dylan wrote numerous songs in this period, apparently without intending to place any of them on albums of his own. "I Shall Be Released" was actually introduced to the public by The Band on their first album, *Music from Big Pink*, in 1968. The song, a verse-chorus number with three strophes, is a kind of secular hymn, a Dylan spiritual without dogma. The shining light that will bring release to the singer remains unspecified in his lyrics. "I Shall Be Released" shares with "All Along the Watchtower" an efficient expression of evocative, yet enigmatic, content. It is not surprising that both songs have achieved wide appeal and have invited a wide range of interpretations—not least in Dylan's own performances of them.

The first two performances of "I Shall Be Released" under consideration here both become vocal duets in the choruses, raising the possibility that this was an aspect of the song's initial conception. Otherwise, the 1967 and 1971 renditions differ strongly in character. Dylan's performance with The Band is stately and measured, emphasizing the seriousness in the lyrics; notice especially the very careful articulation of the title lyrics at the end of every strophe. But the recording with Happy Traum takes a significantly faster tempo and is decidedly upbeat. Despite its official status, the studio version sounds paradoxically much more casual than the earlier unofficial one. Dylan and Traum even omit the first strophe heard in the 1967 performance, making what was a short song to begin with even shorter. A listener could easily imagine the two musicians relaxing and jamming together on a back porch. The half-lazy, half-playful harmonica solos that follow the sung strophes radiate the same spontaneous ambience.

Although musically engaging, the 1971 version might be faulted for removing too much of the song's inherent weightiness. This is, after all, a song that describes high walls and a lonely crowd, a song about a man anticipating some kind of redemption, with another man who cries out that he's been framed. Does the lightness of touch employed by Dylan and Traum ultimately trivialize an important song?

The concert performance of "I Shall Be Released" establishes a moderate tempo and allows for Dylan to be joined in the song's choruses by a female backing group. The result is an anthem-like quality, with the choruses

evoking a gospel sound totally in harmony with the shining light and anticipated salvation envisioned in the lyrics. This selection might be heard to
offer a musical foretaste of the gospel style Dylan would embrace in his
specifically Christian songs soon to come. The three strophes have been
reordered, so that the deeply moving image of the singer seeing his reflec-
tion "so high above this wall" is now positioned in the final strophe. The
chordal vocabulary of the song has been enriched, and an appropriately
intense solo saxophone is heard between the vocal sections. But the most
compelling addition to this version of "I Shall Be Released" is probably the
brief instrumental break that offsets the title words concluding each chorus,
highlighting the affirmation that forms the central focus of this song. At
the end of the performance, the title words are repeated several times with
fervor, the last time a cappella and stretched out in a free tempo. These
performers have clearly seen the light!

I must state in conclusion that this chapter, like others in this book,
scratches the surface of an exceptionally rich area of investigation. Even
the small fraction of Dylan's live performances that, as of 2020, have been
officially released on recordings offer any listener ample opportunities for
delight, surprise, confusion, head-shaking, and disbelief—and sometimes
for several of these reactions simultaneously. Perhaps a headbanging, heavy-
metal-like "Masters of War" makes a certain amount of sense (*Real Live*,
1984). But what about a deceptively gentle, almost lullaby-like approach
to the premonitions expressed in "The Times They Are a-Changin'" (*MTV
Unplugged*, 1995)? Bob Dylan keeps on a-changin', and his wonders show
no signs of ceasing.

9

BRINGING IT ALL BACK HOME

(Pulling It All Together)

The preceding chapters have considered Bob Dylan's artistry from a number of viewpoints. It seems only fitting to conclude by examining a few of his outstanding songs in their totality, as integrated achievements. Any number of songs could serve this purpose in exemplary fashion. I have chosen four that have not so far received any detailed attention and that are representative of Dylan, while being highly distinct from one another—and equally, representative of Dylan *because* they are highly distinct from one another. Exhaustive analyses are not the intent here. The discussions rather will center on some of the ways in which lyrics, musical composition, performance, and arrangement interact in these selections to forge exceptional, and remarkably unified, creations, with each aspect contributing essentially to the impact and significance of the whole.

The first two examples are from the mid-1960s: "Visions of Johanna" from *Blonde on Blonde* (1966), and "Dear Landlord" from *John Wesley Harding* (1967). Both of these reveal Dylan's skill as a composer of strophic songs, as a singer able to employ a wide vocal range to fine expressive effect, and as a musician who makes savvy choices of arrangements and accompanists. But where "Visions of Johanna" is expansive, at points surrealistic, and generous with imagery and metaphor, all leading to a devastating conclusion, "Dear Landlord" is small-scaled, taut, aphoristic, and open-ended.

"Visions of Johanna": Lyrical Panorama, Musical Claustrophobia

"Visions of Johanna" is one of several celebrated Dylan songs from albums released in 1965 and 1966 that are founded on an apparent, but powerful, dichotomy between the lyrics and the music. Although the lyrics range widely and wildly, with a freedom and intensity of language utterly new for their time, the music is constructed from relatively brief, repeated kernels of melody derived from the notes of a single major scale, accompanied by a highly restricted vocabulary of chords. "Mr. Tambourine Man" and "Desolation Row" come readily to mind as additional examples of this dichotomy. In "Visions of Johanna" the uneasy combination accurately depicts the singer's situation: he is "stranded" in an unpleasant room with at least one other person—the mysterious Louise—while his imagination roams elsewhere, longing for escape and for the absent Johanna. Much remains ambiguous in the lyrics, and the music keeps the singer tied down to his obviously limited, oppressive reality. Who is Louise, who is the lover with whom Louise is "so entwined" (some third individual, or perhaps the singer himself?), who is little boy lost (same question—has the singer split himself schizophrenically in two?), who are the peddler and the countess who suddenly appear in the final strophe?—and the questions pile up. Meanwhile, the music relentlessly circles around its short melodic figures and its three chords, trapping the unhappy singer in place.

"Visions of Johanna" is, appropriately, a long song, with five hefty strophes; the last strophe is even prolonged with Dylan's variable strophe technique (see chapter 5). This technique paradoxically provides some variety of structure and underlines with repetitive melody that there really is no relief at all. The accompaniment, consisting of guitars, harmonica, organ, bass, and drums, remains relatively low-key, with only subtle alterations throughout. Musically, this singer will *not* be released.

One musical aspect that does generate considerable interest in "Visions of Johanna" is the shifting of Dylan's vocal melody from lower to higher range, in a marked and systematic fashion. This is evident from the opening line of lyrics, which musically is set as follows:

[low range:] *Ain't it just like the night to play* [sudden jump to much higher range:] *tricks when you're trying to be so quiet?*

In effect, the melody line leaps to a higher octave in mid-phrase. The second line is set in the same way, establishing a pattern:

[low:] *We sit here stranded,* [jump:] *though we're all doin' our best to deny it.*

This deliberately odd breaking of the lines does make a certain kind of sense. The words "play tricks" belong together grammatically, but the leap on *tricks* surely paints the idea well. And the separation in the second line between the "stranded" reality and the attempts at denial also registers meaningfully. What seems most significant to me, however, is the split in the singer's consciousness that is vividly portrayed by this melodic shaping. He is in one place but wishes to be elsewhere. The last two lines of the opening strophe reiterate this melody-to-lyric relationship unambiguously, with the penultimate description of "Louise and her lover" in the high register falling to the final phrase, where the "visions of Johanna" lead the singer to the lowest melody note in the song as they "conquer [his] mind." This split—is it a kind of melodic schizophrenia, mirroring the singer's despairing state of mind?—endures of course throughout the song because of its strophic structure. The final phrase of each strophe presents the song's title words as the singer sinks to his dark low register. It should be emphasized that, by this time in Dylan's career as a songwriter, the strophic form represents a compositional choice on his part, not just a habitual fallback, for a good number of the contemporaneous songs on the *Blonde on Blonde* album have bridge sections.

The strophes in "Visions of Johanna" may be divided into three parts, musically. Continuing with the opening strophe as a model, the first two low-to-high phrases are followed by a transitional phrase that remains in Dylan's higher register ("And Louise holds a handful of rain"), leading to a middle segment with shorter, repeated phrases in a middle register, describing the flickering lights, coughing heating pipes, and country-music radio station that characterize this nightmarish nocturnal scenario. Another transitional, descending phrase ("But there's nothing") brings us to the two concluding lines cited previously. The tripartite structure of the strophes is an important feature, because the repetitive middle segment allows Dylan to suddenly expand the final strophe, building almost unbearable tension as the images and rhymes pile up with the melodic phrases, the singer's unfettered lyrical imagination straining against the apparently stuck, unyielding music. Where the first four strophes had three phrases in their middle segments, the last strophe has six, leading the listener to wonder whether this song will even be permitted an ending. Finally, the singer's conscience "explodes" (along, perhaps, with the listener's effectively strained endurance), and the song ends with the visions of Johanna being "all that remain."

Strophic songs depend on a body of music proving suitable for multiple strophes of lyrics, and although the verbal wealth of this song precludes any thorough discussion along these lines, the first two phrases of the fourth strophe provide further useful illustrations. The fourth strophe stands out for its sudden lyrical leap into the museums, where Mona Lisa is revealed so memorably to have had "the highway blues." In the opening two lines of the strophe, the musical leaps from the singer's low to high register occur on the words *infinity* and *salvation*. I suggest that this pairing of words with music is not mere happenstance.

The instrumental accompaniment in "Visions of Johanna" features Dylan's harmonica in a prominent structural role. It introduces and concludes the song and separates the strophes with brief intervening phrases. The harmonica is also, uniquely, mentioned in the lyrics. The next-to-last, grammatically ambiguous, line is "The harmonicas play the skeleton keys and the rain." Is there a missing or implied period, semicolon, or comma following "harmonicas play"? Or does Dylan intend a musical pun here, with the harmonicas playing in skeleton "keys"? Whatever that might sound like, it would surely suit the haunted environment in "Visions of Johanna." The harmonica-dominated coda follows in short order.

A high-pitched organ enters like a ghostly presence directly after the opening line of lyrics in "Visions of Johanna," setting an appropriately disquieting mood and perhaps mocking the singer's attempt to "be so quiet." Beginning with the second strophe, the electric guitar offers clipped responses to the sung lines. This dialogue reaches a climax during the expanded middle segment of the concluding strophe, as the guitar underlines the accelerating frenzy of the singer's imagery, all while the vocal line and harmony remain stubbornly fixated on their repeating patterns.

"Visions of Johanna" is a major achievement in Bob Dylan's oeuvre. Although every individual aspect of the song—lyrics, musical composition, vocal performance, instrumental arrangement, and instrumental performance—is admirable in its own right, it is the synthesis of these elements that makes the song a truly distinctive and distinguished accomplishment.

"Dear Landlord": Moving or Staying?

If "Visions of Johanna" is a musical study in confinement, adhering melodically to a single scale and harmonically to three chords, "Dear Landlord" ventures far and wide musically within its much shorter time span. The song is unusual in several respects. Dylan's piano accompaniment sets it apart from the surrounding tracks on *John Wesley Harding*. (The only other selection on the album in which Dylan's piano is heard is "Down Along the Cove.") And the lyrical subject matter, articulating the singer's relationship to some unidentified authority figure—the landlord remains unnamed and unspecified—offers no unambiguous analogy to other songs in Dylan's output.

The efficient piano introduction grounds "Dear Landlord" on its tonic major chord, which is necessary for a song that will so soon move out of that chord's orbit. The originality and expressivity of "Dear Landlord" stems as much from its melodic and harmonic adventurousness as it does from the character of its verbal expression. By the end of the second line of lyrics, the vocal melody has already ventured out of scale, and the accompanying harmony has ventured out of key, as the singer asks the landlord not to "put a price on [his] *soul.*" The unexpected, weighty word virtually demands a musical parallel (or vice versa). This then leads into minor-key territory, as the singer recounts his heavy burden and his uncontrollable dreams.

Further surprises ensue, verbally and musically. A new, high-register chromatic pitch enters the vocal line as, from out of nowhere, a steamboat whistle *blows*, and melody and harmony shift out of key again as the line ascends rapidly into its stratosphere, Dylan's voice rising to a shout with the effort of giving the landlord *all* he has to give. The melody gradually falls for the last two lines of the strophe, but without achieving resolution. The singer can only hope that the landlord will receive his "all" appropriately and stops short of the tonic note, ending on the second scale degree. The piano provides a two-chord turnaround to prepare the tonic chord, which returns only with the start of the next strophe. Thus, the strophes are linked musically to one another and become part of an essential continuity within the song as a whole. Dylan the composer will utilize this feature tellingly when he comes to conclude the song.

The remarkable synergy of words and music endures for the remaining two strophes of "Dear Landlord." All three strophes feature a second line of lyrics that begins with "please" and ends with a crucial word to mark the change of harmony (or vice versa); following "soul" in this position are "words that I *speak*" and "dismiss my *case*." In an analogous position to "blows" in the initial strophe are "too *hard*" and "special *gift*," in the second and third strophes, respectively. And the striking melodic ascent to the highest vocal register highlights central lyrics in each stanza: "to have it too fast and too much" the second time around (especially fitting, with the rapid rhythmic values in the passage) and finally "you know this was meant to be true." Ending the song without a fade-out, the last strophe stops necessarily on an inconclusive chord (in technical terms, the dominant, the chord built on the fifth degree of the scale), since there is no strophe to follow and provide the missing tonic. This rather startling open ending underlines the essential issue that the lyrics leave hanging as well, namely, that *if* the landlord doesn't underestimate the singer, then the singer won't underestimate the landlord. Yes, *if*, but only if. There is no certainty here, lyrically or musically.

The vacillating, wandering character of the music in "Dear Landlord" perfectly embodies the equivocations expressed in the lyrics. Whereas in the initial strophe the singer refers to a "steamboat whistle," presumably calling him away, in the concluding strophe he asserts to the landlord that he is not about to move anywhere else. If "Visions of Johanna" fixes its visionary protagonist in an oppressively defined place and time, "Dear Landlord," in complete contrast, finds its philosophical protagonist in an uncertain position at, and for, an unspecified period.

Bob Dylan as a Late-Period Romantic: "Life Is Hard" and "This Dream of You"

The other two songs for consideration here both come from the album *Together through Life* (2009), released more than forty years after *John Wesley Harding*. "Life Is Hard" and "This Dream of You" share a number of features. The lyrics are very personal in nature (Robert Hunter is credited as colyricist for "Life Is Hard"), expressing the deep romantic yearning of "I" for an absent "you": in the former song, "life is hard/Without you near me"; in the latter, "All I have and all I know/Is this dream of you." Dylan's obviously aged voice, in evidence throughout *Together through Life*, contributes strongly to the poignancy of his performances. From a formal standpoint, both songs have bridge sections, a factor that might suggest a kinship to sentimental songs of earlier periods. But these Dylan songs share a distinction from many other songs of sentiment, insofar as the "you" being longed for in these instances is given no defining physical characteristics. The nature of the singer's feelings could hardly be more explicit, although the object of those feelings remains a matter of speculation for the listener.

Despite the many similarities, "Life Is Hard" and "This Dream of You" are decisively different in effect from one another. Melody, harmony, rhythm, nuances in Dylan's singing, and musical instrumentation and arrangement all contribute to the making of highly individual performances.

"Life Is Hard" opens with an instrumental introduction that is as concise as it is arresting. The immediately prominent mandolin sets a gentle, lyrical tone, reinforced by the steel guitar, but rendered somewhat restless by the constantly modulating harmony that underlies it. This music prepares the delicate expression of deep dissatisfaction that will characterize the song as a whole. The introduction ends by arriving on what seems like a tonic major chord, but the momentary impression of stability is instantly and startlingly destabilized by the opening vocal pitch and its accompanying harmony. This vocal entrance is musically one of the most expressive moments in any Dylan song, and it achieves its impact largely because of the deceptive context established by the preceding introduction.

The melody line, beginning high in Dylan's register, scarcely moves at first, depicting the "still" evening winds, but that surprising opening pitch and its totally unexpected harmonization alert us immediately to the presence of something amiss. This song will not be celebrating a peaceful nature scene. Indeed, the vocal phrases proceed to descend steadily as the singer describes his loss of "way and will," and the chords change restlessly, echoing that aspect of the introduction, suggesting first one key and then another. It is only with the final words of the opening stanza, "without you near me," that the voice and harmony arrive at, and confirm, the tonic note and tonic chord suggested in the introduction. Yet here is another kind of expressive paradox, for this point of musical rest offers only a confirmation of absence.

Over the course of this first stanza, Dylan's voice descends from the highest melodic pitch in the song to the lowest, over a range of nearly two octaves. Dylan adopts a crooning approach, appropriate to the tenderness and weariness of the sentiments, and his drawing out of the final, drastically low notes of his line is particularly moving, with the pain in his voice truly palpable. The vocal phrases begin almost always off the beat and are characterized by steady, plodding motion, articulating in rhythmic terms the singer's reluctance, and limited ability, to move forward. Eventually, the slow, walking rhythms gain a lyrical corollary, as the singer comes to "pass the old schoolyard" and "walk the boulevard."

As the voice begins the second stanza, the accompaniment joins the trudging rhythms, underlining the words "The friend you used to be/So near and dear to me." Then, as it is sung that the friend "slipped so far away," the mandolin also slips away from the singer and becomes more independent. This subtle but telling expressive detail is typical of the sensitivity brought to "Life Is Hard" by Dylan's fellow musicians. The mandolin and steel guitar are especially and consistently responsive to the lyrical and musical thrust of his vocals.

After the second stanza is the bridge section of this A-A-B-A-A form, in which the lyrics become more revealing of the reason for the separation. The friend did not simply slip away, rather the friend *went* away. The new melodic line serves to articulate this important difference. The accompaniment meanwhile reiterates the chord progressions of the introduction, so that the bridge becomes a source of both variety and unity in the song's overall structure. The introduction music is played twice through in the bridge, with a singular and significant modification. The final chord of this section is *not* the expected tonic. This makes the chord that comes with the return of the A music even more of a dislocation, in terms of harmony.

While "Life Is Hard" could seem formally complete without the additional A section at the end, Dylan certainly makes the most of this extra stanza, verbally and musically. The lyrics return us to a natural setting, with the sinking sun, but the still evening winds of the opening have now been replaced by a "chilly breeze." The voice concludes its melody, and the instruments undertake a final presentation of the introduction music. But this seemingly straightforward rounding gesture becomes something else, as Dylan begins to hum unexpectedly and then sings, yet again, and in perfect synchrony with the now-familiar chord progression, "Without you near me." He draws out "you" as if unwilling to let go. And finally, the instruments decorate the last chord with a melodic flourish and added chord tones, ending with gentle but obvious dissonance that beautifully encapsulates the emotional essence of "Life Is Hard."

"This Dream of You" also opens with a brief instrumental introduction, establishing its totally different musical and emotional ambience as efficiently as the passage that begins "Life Is Hard." The violin and the accordion are the two immediately noticeable ensemble members here, fulfilling roles parallel to those played by the mandolin and the steel guitar in "Life Is Hard," creating a distinctive atmosphere. The accordion contributes something of a Cajun flavor, helping to situate the "nowhere café" in the opening line of lyrics. The relaxed tempo and conventional harmony suggest rather an upbeat, unproblematic mood—were it not for the oddly placed drum accents that quite literally kick in with the first full bar of music and that wind up persisting throughout the entire performance. In this case it is the rhythm that alerts us to something askew. In the four-beat measures of "This Dream of You," the drum consistently pounds at half-past two (midway between beats two and three). The drum seems out of place, which turns out to be true of the singer as well, who enters this environment with a downbeat tale of despair, having only his "dream of you" to keep him living.

The lyrics radiate scant hope for a reunion with the absent one. The singer is "frightened of dawn"; his moment of renewal "might have been here and gone," gone along with all his friends; even a fleeting symbol of hope, a shooting star, is also now gone. How is this hopelessness reflected in the song's music? There are some indications, but the core feeling is that of a dichotomy between the basic flavor of the instrumental music and that of the sung lyrics. In this regard, "This Dream of You" lies at the opposite expressive pole from "Life Is Hard," yet it may be equally effective in a different way. The dichotomy in "This Dream of You" reflects the utter isolation of the singer from the external world in which he finds himself. The superficially cheerful music functions ironically, underlining the singer's deep hurt and alienation in a paradoxical way by refusing ultimately to respond to it. The occasional, limited exceptions only reinforce the fundamental irony.

The prominent exceptions come in the song's two bridge sections. The overall form is A-A-B-A-B-A, with an added instrumental A section before the second bridge, in which the steel guitar joins the violin as a leading melody instrument. Each bridge is marked by a new turn in the lyrics— first, "I look away"; second, more drastically, "Everything I touch seems to disappear." In the latter half of each bridge, the harmony abruptly turns away from the traditional three-chord vocabulary that prevails everywhere else. Minor coloring reflects the shadows dancing on the wall in the first bridge, and there is a brief but striking, chromatic descending bass line here as well. The parallel music in the second bridge accompanies the only specific lyrical references to death. But the instruments inevitably return to their major-key music. Their apparent obliviousness to the singer's anguish becomes especially poignant in the final stanza, as the singer describes his "cheerless room in a curtained gloom."

Dylan's vocal line in "This Dream of You" is characteristic in its reliance on repeated notes. The brevity of many phrases leads, however, to extensive vocal silences, which become as expressive as the singing itself in representing the singer's physical and emotional immobility. The vocal pauses are particularly noticeable in the bridge sections and after the words "all I have" and "all I know" in each of the A sections. Whenever Dylan sings "all I have" and "all I know," his vocal syncopations on "have" and "know" align with the drum accents, a synchrony that takes place at other points in the song (such as in the opening line: "How long can I *stay* in this nowhere *café*"). If a listener chooses to hear the drum as a dislocated kindred spirit to the singer in the musical environment of "This Dream of You," these instances reinforce that conception.

"Life Is Hard" and "This Dream of You" attest to the continuing power, and even novelty, of Bob Dylan's inspiration as songwriter and performer. These two late songs, so different from one another in conception and in execution, show that his capacity to surprise and enrich his listeners surpasses expectations at every turn.

ACKNOWLEDGMENTS

As I complete this exploration of Bob Dylan's work, I am struck by a singular revelation. I could begin this book all over again, with the same goals and conceptual framework, and even all the same chapter headings, and utilize a totally different collection of Dylan songs for discussion and illustration. The result would be equally valid as a testament to Dylan's artistry. Such is the breadth and richness of the man's work.

I must conclude by thanking those people who have contributed so much to making this book possible. I have taught courses on popular music throughout my academic career, including a seminar specifically on the music of Bob Dylan, and have always learned more from my students than they could have learned from me. My research assistant, scholar, and performer Sarah Kolat provided invaluable assistance in many ways, particularly on matters related to vocal performance. John Hanford and Tom Collier, musician colleagues at the University of Washington, made themselves consistently available for consultations about Dylan's music. I am also grateful to Seattle musicians Orville Johnson, guitarist, and Grant Dermody, harmonica virtuoso, for sharing their wisdom about Dylan as a performer on their favored instruments.

My wife of more than five decades, Leslie, is an unending source of support for my work and of love and comfort. My gratitude to her is boundless. John and Trina Brenes are the owners of my favorite independent record store, Music Coop in Ashland, Oregon, which has been a remarkable and generous source of Dylan and Dylan-related recordings both celebrated and obscure, and I thank them also for much stimulating conversation about all matters Dylan.

Finally, I owe Laurie Matheson, director of the University of Illinois Press, my deep thanks. Her enthusiasm and her support for this project, from its earliest conception, have been profound and unwavering. I thank also Ms. Matheson's excellent staff at the University of Illinois Press for shepherding this book through the many details of prepublication and publication: astute copyeditor Geof Garvey, enthusiastic project manager Tad Ringo, book designer Jennifer Fisher, catalog and copywriting coordinator Kevin Cunningham, marketing assistant Roberta Sparenberg, and compositor Kirsten Dennison. The essential and well-designed indexes were produced by the most diligent Judy Lyon Davis. The readers of my manuscript-in-progress for the Press offered constructive and insightful suggestions, all of which improved my finished product. As for that product, the flaws and limitations that remain are strictly my own doing. And now, as Bob Dylan sang in his own "Restless Farewell," "it's closing time / So I'll bid farewell and be down the road."

A VERY SELECTIVE BIBLIOGRAPHY

The literature on Bob Dylan is voluminous, but very little of it approaches the music in a detailed manner or with the range of this book. Consequently, the following list is limited to printed books that I have personally found directly relevant to my own work, and a few other recent volumes that might engage a reader seeking to broaden her perspective on Bob Dylan. The Margotin and Guesdon *Bob Dylan: All the Songs* proved particularly useful for ascertaining the musicians employed and the production history of many of the recordings discussed.

Bell, Ian. *Once upon a Time: The Lives of Bob Dylan*. New York: Pegasus, 2012.

Burger, Jeff, ed. *Dylan on Dylan: Interviews and Encounters*. Chicago: Chicago Review Press, 2018.

Cott, Jonathan, ed. *Bob Dylan: The Essential Interviews*. New York: Simon and Schuster, 2017.

Dylan, Bob. *Chronicles, Volume One*. New York: Simon and Schuster, 2004.

———. *The Definitive Bob Dylan Songbook*. Edited by Don Giller and Ed Lozano. New York: Amsco, 2001.

———. *The Lyrics*. Edited by Christopher Ricks, Lisa Nemrow, and Julie Nemrow. New York: Simon and Schuster, 2014.

———. *The Lyrics: 1961–2012*. New York: Simon and Schuster, 2016.

———. *The Nobel Lecture*. New York: Simon and Schuster, 2017.

Field, Kim. *Harmonicas, Harps, and Heavy Breathers: The Evolution of the People's Instrument*. Updated ed. New York: Cooper Square, 2000.

Gill, Andy, and Kevin Odegard. *A Simple Twist of Fate: Bob Dylan and the Making of "Blood on the Tracks."* Cambridge, MA: Da Capo, 2004.

Gray, Michael. *Song and Dance Man III: The Art of Bob Dylan*. London: Continuum, 2000.

Hedin, Benjamin, ed. *Studio A: The Bob Dylan Reader*. New York: W. W. Norton, 2004.

Heylin, Clinton. *Bob Dylan: Behind the Shades Revisited*. New York: HarperCollins, 2001.

———. *Bob Dylan: The Recording Sessions, 1960–1994*. New York: St. Martin's Griffin, 1995.

———. *Revolution in the Air: The Songs of Bob Dylan, 1957–1973*. Chicago: Chicago Review Press, 2009.

———. *Still on the Road: The Songs of Bob Dylan, 1974–2006*. Chicago: Chicago Review Press, 2010.

Kozinn, Alan, et al. *The Guitar: The History, the Music, the Players*. New York: Quill, 1984.

Marcus, Greil. *Bob Dylan by Greil Marcus: Writings 1968–2010*. New York: PublicAffairs, 2010.

———. *Like a Rolling Stone: Bob Dylan at the Crossroads*. New York: Public Affairs, 2006.

———. *The Old, Weird America: The World of Bob Dylan's Basement Tapes*. New York: Picador, 2011.

Margotin, Philippe, and Jean-Michel Guesdon. *Bob Dylan: All the Songs*. New York: Black Dog and Leventhal, 2015.

Negus, Keith. *Bob Dylan*. Bloomington: Indiana University Press, 2008.

Polizzotti, Mark. *Highway 61 Revisited*. New York: Continuum, 2006.

Ricks, Christopher. *Dylan's Visions of Sin*. New York: Ecco, 2004.

Shelton, Robert, Elizabeth Thomson, and Patrick Humphries. *No Direction Home: The Life and Music of Bob Dylan*. Rev. ed. Milwaukee, WI: Backbeat, 2011.

Sounes, Howard. *Down the Highway: The Life of Bob Dylan*. Rev. ed. New York: Grove, 2011.

Thomson, Elizabeth, and David Gutman, eds. *The Dylan Companion*. Cambridge, MA: Da Capo, 2001.

Wilentz, Sean. *Bob Dylan in America*. New York: Doubleday, 2010.

SUBJECT INDEX

Also please see separate Song Index.

SONG INDEX

LARRY STARR is emeritus professor of music history at the University of Washington. He is the author of *George Gershwin* and coauthor of *American Popular Music: From Minstrelsy to MP3*, sixth edition.

MUSIC IN AMERICAN LIFE

John Alden Carpenter: A Chicago Composer   *Howard Pollack*
Heartbeat of the People: Music and Dance of the Northern Pow-wow
    Tara Browner
My Lord, What a Morning: An Autobiography   *Marian Anderson*
Marian Anderson: A Singer's Journey   *Allan Keiler*
Charles Ives Remembered: An Oral History   *Vivian Perlis*
Henry Cowell, Bohemian   *Michael Hicks*
Rap Music and Street Consciousness   *Cheryl L. Keyes*
Louis Prima   *Garry Boulard*
Marian McPartland's Jazz World: All in Good Time   *Marian McPartland*
Robert Johnson: Lost and Found   *Barry Lee Pearson and Bill McCulloch*
Bound for America: Three British Composers   *Nicholas Temperley*
Lost Sounds: Blacks and the Birth of the Recording Industry, 1890–1919
    Tim Brooks
Burn, Baby! BURN! The Autobiography of Magnificent Montague
    Magnificent Montague with Bob Baker
Way Up North in Dixie: A Black Family's Claim to the Confederate Anthem
    Howard L. Sacks and Judith Rose Sacks
The Bluegrass Reader   *Edited by Thomas Goldsmith*
Colin McPhee: Composer in Two Worlds   *Carol J. Oja*
Robert Johnson, Mythmaking, and Contemporary American Culture
    Patricia R. Schroeder
Composing a World: Lou Harrison, Musical Wayfarer   *Leta E. Miller and*
    Fredric Lieberman
Fritz Reiner, Maestro and Martinet   *Kenneth Morgan*
That Toddlin' Town: Chicago's White Dance Bands
    and Orchestras, 1900–1950   *Charles A. Sengstock Jr.*
Dewey and Elvis: The Life and Times of a Rock 'n' Roll Deejay
    Louis Cantor
Come Hither to Go Yonder: Playing Bluegrass with Bill Monroe   *Bob Black*
Chicago Blues: Portraits and Stories   *David Whiteis*
The Incredible Band of John Philip Sousa   *Paul E. Bierley*
"Maximum Clarity" and Other Writings on Music   *Ben Johnston,*
    edited by Bob Gilmore
Staging Tradition: John Lair and Sarah Gertrude Knott
    Michael Ann Williams
Homegrown Music: Discovering Bluegrass   *Stephanie P. Ledgin*
Tales of a Theatrical Guru   *Danny Newman*
The Music of Bill Monroe   *Neil V. Rosenberg and Charles K. Wolfe*
Pressing On: The Roni Stoneman Story   *Roni Stoneman, as told to*
    Ellen Wright

Gone to the Country: The New Lost City Ramblers and the
Folk Music Revival   *Ray Allen*

The Makers of the Sacred Harp   *David Warren Steel with Richard H. Hulan*

Woody Guthrie, American Radical   *Will Kaufman*

George Szell: A Life of Music   *Michael Charry*

Bean Blossom: The Brown County Jamboree and Bill Monroe's
Bluegrass Festivals   *Thomas A. Adler*

Crowe on the Banjo: The Music Life of J. D. Crowe   *Marty Godbey*

Twentieth Century Drifter: The Life of Marty Robbins   *Diane Diekman*

Henry Mancini: Reinventing Film Music   *John Caps*

The Beautiful Music All Around Us: Field Recordings and
the American Experience   *Stephen Wade*

Then Sings My Soul: The Culture of Southern Gospel Music
Douglas Harrison

The Accordion in the Americas: Klezmer, Polka, Tango, Zydeco, and More!
Edited by Helena Simonett

Bluegrass Bluesman: A Memoir   *Josh Graves, edited by Fred Bartenstein*

One Woman in a Hundred: Edna Phillips and the Philadelphia Orchestra
Mary Sue Welsh

The Great Orchestrator: Arthur Judson and American Arts Management
James M. Doering

Charles Ives in the Mirror: American Histories of an Iconic Composer
David C. Paul

Southern Soul-Blues   *David Whiteis*

Sweet Air: Modernism, Regionalism, and American Popular Song
Edward P. Comentale

Pretty Good for a Girl: Women in Bluegrass   *Murphy Hicks Henry*

Sweet Dreams: The World of Patsy Cline   *Warren R. Hofstra*

William Sidney Mount and the Creolization of American Culture
Christopher J. Smith

Bird: The Life and Music of Charlie Parker   *Chuck Haddix*

Making the March King: John Philip Sousa's Washington Years, 1854–1893
Patrick Warfield

In It for the Long Run   *Jim Rooney*

Pioneers of the Blues Revival   *Steve Cushing*

Roots of the Revival: American and British Folk Music in the 1950s
Ronald D. Cohen and Rachel Clare Donaldson

Blues All Day Long: The Jimmy Rogers Story   *Wayne Everett Goins*

Yankee Twang: Country and Western Music in New England
Clifford R. Murphy

The Music of the Stanley Brothers   *Gary B. Reid*

The University of Illinois Press
is a founding member of the
Association of University Presses.

———————————————

Composed in 10.25/14 Chaparral Pro
with Abraham and Insignia display
by Kirsten Dennison
at the University of Illinois Press
Manufactured by Sheridan Books, Inc.

University of Illinois Press
1325 South Oak Street
Champaign, IL 61820-6903
www.press.uillinois.edu